Casper the Commuting Cat

Casper the Commuting Cat

Susan Finden

**SIMON &
SCHUSTER**

London · New York · Sydney · Toronto

A CBS COMPANY

First published in Great Britain by Simon & Schuster UK Ltd, 2010
This edition published in Great Britain by
Simon & Schuster UK Ltd, 20011
A CBS Company

9 10 8

Simon & Schuster UK Ltd
1st Floor
222 Gray's Inn Road
London WC1X 8HB

www.simonandschuster.co.uk

Simon & Schuster Australia
Sydney

A CIP catalogue record for this book is available
from the British Library.

ISBN: 978-1-84983-175-8

Typeset by Hewer Text UK Ltd, Edinburgh
Printed and bound by CPI Group (UK) Ltd, Croydon, CR0 4YY

This book is dedicated to you, the readers, because its proceeds will help assist unfortunate animals. It is also written in memory, of course, of our best friend and lovely old gentleman, Casper.

Contents

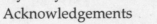

Prologue

This is the story of a cat – one little cat. There are other stories of other cats woven into it, but everything revolves around Casper. If it weren't for him, there would be no book. If it weren't for him, there would be no story.

You may have heard of my cat. If you have, you'll be in the company of hundreds of thousands of others across the world. One day, Casper left his house, got on a bus and stole the hearts of the nation. As the tale of the travelling cat spread, his fame spread too. It made no difference to Casper. He expected the good things in life – a warm seat on the bus, a nice meal when he got home, a cuddle when he settled down for the night. He was oblivious to the maelstrom of attention that was swirling around him.

Life was good for Casper. It hadn't always been that way, but ever since I'd rescued him, years before his name hit the headlines, he had been happy and loved. He brought so much to my life and to the lives of others.

If you know about Casper, you will also know how the story ends – and that is where it has to start. I must be honest with you – as I write this book, as I dip into my treasure trove of memories, the tears are flowing. Why? Because I have lost my beautiful cat. I've lost Casper.

Some people will scoff; some will say that I have no sense of perspective, breaking my heart over the death of 'just' a cat. Well, they're wrong. Casper wasn't *just* a cat; to me, he was one of the most amazing, individual creatures who ever lived. From the day he came into my life until the day he left it, I knew I'd been blessed with a feline character I would never forget. I had no way of knowing that this bundle of fluff and mischief would touch so many other people too. Not only would he change my world, he would reach out across the globe and remind people what truly matters.

In this day and age, we are so used to hearing terrible things, to witnessing heartbreaking stories on the news – sometimes feeling there is nothing but doom and gloom everywhere – we often respond to anything that offers some respite. That is what Casper offered. As the astounding tale of the cat who travelled the bus hit the headlines in every country, something astonishing and rather wonderful happened: people opened their hearts.

This is Casper's story, but it is also the story of every one of us who has loved an animal. We may sometimes wonder why we feel so strongly for these creatures who share our lives, but I truly believe that our capacity to love and care for our fellow creatures is something we should cling to and take pride in. If Casper has accomplished anything, it has been that he has brought people together – a remarkable achievement for one little cat.

My tears may still be flowing, for I can't deny that there is a terrible gap in my life where Casper used to be, but I'm smiling too. I hope you'll join me in the rollercoaster of emotion as I share the incredible tale of Casper the Commuting Cat.

With love – Sue x

My Story

Casper

🐾

Sue is quite right when she says this is the story of a cat
called Casper. It *is* my story, and I'm delighted it's being
told, as I certainly made the most of my life. Whilst a
lot of my fellow cats were happy to observe their owner's
boundaries, I always went that bit further. Inquisitiveness
is in a cat's nature but for me it was everything. I simply
had to climb that fence, jump over that wall or ride that
bus. There was just so much exploring to do. Of course,
thinking back, I wish I'd not have been quite as nosy and
naughty. If I hadn't insisted on going out that January
morning I might still be down there with the rest of you,
eating tasty treats. But I lived my nine lives the only way
I could - to the full. And now I'm on the other side, across
the rainbow bridge - as the afterlife is called in the animal
world - I can look back with a sense of satisfaction that I
went to places few cats are bold enough to explore.

I hope you don't mind, but I'd like to point out a few
things about what it's like for a cat trying to make his way

around that crazy planet of yours. We felines can sometimes feel a little bemused by it all. You see, humans, while often acting with the best of intentions, do have some peculiar ways. I'm sure most of you conduct yourself as well as you can, but there are so many rules and regulations, that I often wonder how you get from day to day. You rush around, always in a hurry, always so concerned about things that seem - may I say - rather unimportant, yet when creatures such as myself try to slow you down, to make you see the pleasant things in life, you are generally amenable, which means there is hope for you. How much easier each day would be if you took a few lessons from us cats and tried to see things the furry way.

While I was quite content to make new friends, explore new worlds and embark on adventures, there were moments when I found your world quite crazy. That got me thinking how useful it would be if there were guidelines to make the journey and the relationships clearer.

Which brings me to this: the next time you wonder where your cat companion has been for the day, instead of asking daft questions that no self-respecting member of the cat world would ever answer, even if we could talk, it would save us all a lot of time if you were simply to refer to Casper's Rules, which I have reproduced in this book for the benefit of all. My time on earth may have passed, but there is no reason why I cannot still teach you a better way of doing things. I do hope that, in return, you will learn.

I hope you enjoy my tales of how I managed to navigate this strange place - the conventions I needed to understand

(and sometimes avoid), as well as the various tricks I used
to ensure humans realized just how important it was for me
to go about my daily business as effortlessly as possible. I
may no longer be with you physically, but I'm still around.
I'm still here to help and guide you. I am, after all, rather
fond of you.

So now it's time to enter my world ... with a little help
from my mum.

Casper

CHAPTER 1

Finding Casper

There was a time before Casper, but I can barely remember it. When I look back on my life, it's full of cats and cat memories, but Casper was so special and so unforgettable that he is the one who seems to colour so much of what I recall.

It will surprise no one when I say that I love cats. I've had so many over the years that you may think I must have lost count, but that's far from true. I remember every one, every name, every character.

They all have their individual traits – in this they are no different from their human companions – and they all give so much in return for the love and care we offer them. When we cry, they come to us. When we laugh, they suddenly appear to see what all the fuss is about. When we need a break or a distraction, they decide that it's time they had some attention or some food. When we feel stress, that's often when they drop a toy at our feet, or start chasing their own tail, or decide to sit on

our desk. They are the most intuitive creatures imaginable, always aware of what would help us.

That's not to say they are selfless – far from it. In fact,
if you want your cat to be particularly responsive to
what may help you, it's a good idea to make sure kitty
has everything he or she needs first. I've found that
once they have all that is deemed necessary in their
little world, they're a lot more conscientious about what
mum or dad may want too. When that happens, you'll
find no more loyal a friend.

There has been many an occasion when I've had bad
news or felt rather down, and before I knew it, a cat
would be beside me, purring contentedly as if to reassure me someone would always be there when needed.
Cats recognize happiness too, and can always be relied
upon to respond to a joyful atmosphere, as if their little
paws would happily dance around in joy to mirror your
own.

Over the years, my cats have given me so much. They
all contributed something to my life, and they all had
their own special traits and idiosyncrasies. Something
about Casper was different, however. I've adored the
feline family I've accumulated over the years, but something about that little chap touched me the moment I
saw him, and it continues to affect me every single day.
Maybe there *is* someone for everyone. We all hope to
find another person whom we can love and share our
life with, and perhaps that applies to pets too. So often
there is simply a connection that can't be explained; it's

one of the luckiest coincidences in the world. To find another creature we connect with is a precious thing. I've experienced that connection with all of my cats, but especially so with Casper.

There was nothing particularly momentous about the day I went to collect him. My husband Chris has the patience of a saint and is used to me deciding on a whim to get another cat. To his great credit, he's always supportive and gets the car ready for us to set off at the right time. The practical aspects are left to him, and I appreciate that hugely. I'm the one who makes the emotional, almost instantaneous, decision that another bundle of fur is coming to live with us.

I've had all ages and types of cats over the years, but as I've grown older myself, I've gone for 'geriatrics' – they're much harder to home because most people tend to want cute kittens. Older cats often have health problems, but I love the idea of giving everyone a chance and making sure that the last days of some poor animals' lives are filled with comfort and love. Maybe, as the years pass, I hope that someone will care for me that way too.

I've had many jobs working with the elderly and with adults who have learning difficulties. These people all have special needs and they have as much right to be treated with respect as anyone else. That has, no doubt, rubbed off on me and affected how I view the world. Not only do I want humans to have some dignity in their final years, but I also want that to extend to animals.

I am as soppy as anyone else when faced with a six-week-old kitten looking up at me with huge eyes, and my heartstrings are tugged in just the same way, but I know that kitten will find a home so much more easily than a ten-year-old cat with arthritis, or one that has only a year or so to live because of terminal cancer. By taking in the older waifs and strays I hope to be able to right some of the wrongs that have been done to them over the years. In giving them love and care during their final days, I get a great deal of pleasure and satisfaction myself. It isn't an unhappy option: there are plenty of laughs and cuddles, and I feel blessed by every single paw that trots through my door.

One day, in December 2002, I did my usual thing of telling Chris, 'It's time to get another cat.' I haven't always had such a supportive husband, and there is part of me that is in awe every time Chris goes along with my plans. Patiently, yet again, he agreed – and didn't bat an eyelid when I said that, actually, I thought two would be a good idea. Indeed, for most people, two may very well have been an excellent notion, but for us perhaps it wasn't the best proposal. Getting sibling cats or two who have known each other from a rescue centre means that they always have a playmate, there's always someone to keep them company, but that wasn't going to be a problem in our house, as we had six cats already.

At the time, we were living in a beautiful three-storey Victorian villa in Weymouth, Dorset. The house was huge, with lots of space, a secluded garden and a cellar – plenty of places for inquisitive kitties to hide and explore. We tend to move house quite frequently and I am always on the lookout for a home that is cat-friendly. This one ticked most of the boxes. The property was big enough for the cats to roam freely, and to go out or stay in according to their temperament. I never felt that the place was overflowing.

When I had the desire to bring more cats into the family, it didn't seem a problem. I love to be surrounded by cats, and I would happily take on more and more until they were everywhere. I have enough love to go around, but I will house another cat only if we have the financial capacity to feed and care for him or her. Older cats need a great deal of veterinary care, and those costs must always be taken into consideration by anyone who is expanding their family. Love is one of the main qualifications when acquiring any pet, but money helps too. If I had a bottomless pit of cash, I would have an endless troupe of cats; as it is, I must be practical and realize that these ill and old pets might often cause me to dip into my resources.

As well as giving a home to older cats, I always make sure I get them from rescue centres, usually ones affiliated with Cats Protection. I know charities face problems getting 'forever homes' for these feline pensioners, so I tend to keep in touch with them whenever we move into a new area. By the time I feel the need to get a new cat, I've usually built up a relationship with the organizer.

'Come on then, Sue,' called Chris on the morning we were heading off to get the cats. 'Let's go see what we're getting this time.' We had no idea who we were going to opt for, as I hadn't chatted with the lady who housed them, and both Chris and I left with an open mind, telling the cats we left behind that we'd be coming home with some new playmates for them.

Off we drove on the empty Sunday roads to meet Casper, without realizing what was going to happen to our lives. In retrospect, I wonder how I would have felt had I known that I was about to welcome into my world the cat who would change it. As with most momentous changes, I was blissfully unaware, thinking of nothing more than the happiness I always felt in welcoming a new animal into our home.

This particular cat home was linked to Cats Protection but it was a private house rather than a shelter. It was run by an elderly lady in an impressive 1930s property, which she shared with the cats. She lived upstairs and eighteen cats had the run of the downstairs.

When she invited us in, we were immediately surrounded by all these creatures, sniffing us and rubbing against us. They were clearly perfectly happy, even though they were pretty much left to their own devices. They were all mixed together but there was a very relaxed atmosphere. While we there, I wasn't aware of any fighting, hissing or spitting – which seemed a good omen. The house was big enough for them to have their own space if they wanted it, or to hang around with a friend if they preferred. The only problem for us was going to be how to choose from the many cats there. Chris and I had taken two wicker cat baskets with us, and there was no way I was leaving without my new companions.

The lady said it was feeding time and we followed her through to the kitchen, where there were stainless steel dishes, for water and meat and crunchy snacks, dotted around everywhere. She put enough food into each bowl to feed four cats, although it was a bit of a squeeze. We stood there watching them, hoping for inspiration or for one of them to come over to us.

After a little while, Chris nudged my arm with his elbow and raised his eyebrows towards the window sill. We both looked over and the cat lady noticed. 'Oh, that's Tuppence,' she said, indicating a big white cat with black markings and the most beautiful blue-green eyes. 'He's a lovely boy,' she continued, 'very inquisitive and friendly. He came from an elderly gentleman who loved Siamese cats and Tuppence was the only one who wasn't that breed. I think he must have a bit of Siamese in him though, because his eyes look exactly the same. He'd be perfect for you.' We both thought so too. I liked the way he was watching everyone, biding his time until things calmed down. I agreed that he would be ideal, but whom else should we take?

'He's got a friend, you know,' said the lady, as we picked Tuppence up and popped him into the basket.

'Come on now, Morse, where are you?' she chatted, looking around at the cats on the work surfaces.

'Morse?' I asked.

She laughed as she explained to me that this fellow had arrived at her door one evening as she was watching *Inspector Morse* on TV and she'd thought it was a sign that she should call him Morse. The name jarred with me straight away. As soon as she pointed out the beautiful long-haired black and white cat eating his lunch, I knew he needed a new name – I also knew he was the one for me. If you've ever chosen a pet, you'll know there are some animals you simply connect with immediately. I felt it the moment I looked at 'Morse'. I glanced over at Chris.

'What do you think?' I asked.

'It's up to you,' he said. 'He certainly is a very good-looking cat.'

I went over to stroke him and he started to purr. 'Hello, my darling,' I whispered. 'How would you like to come and live with us?' He nuzzled into my shoulder as I picked him up and walked to the cat basket. When we got there, we found another cat had taken up residence.

'Come on, Georgina,' shooed the lady. 'That's not for you; you're staying here with me.' My heart sank. The poor little thing had clambered in; she clearly thought she was coming home with us.

'Tuppence and Morse will be perfect together,' the lady said. 'Morse has been here for ten months. I don't know why no one has taken him. He's a lovely cat. So many people seemed on the verge of giving him a home then changed their minds at the last minute.'

I looked at Georgina in the basket but, listening to the cat lady's words, I couldn't help feeling that Morse had been waiting for us. As we walked out with him and Tuppence, I felt such a pang for the cat we'd left behind. To this day I regret not taking her, but even at the time I knew we had two new boys in our lives who were perfect for us.

When we got back to Weymouth, the cats shot upstairs as soon as we let them out. Over the course of the day, it became clear that Tuppence was a dreadful bag of nerves, although he seemed to crave affection from us.

As for Morse – well, that cat was one for the vanishing act! He wouldn't come out from under the bed no matter what I tried – not even for food. I called his name. I made smoochy noises. I told him how the other cats desperately wanted to meet him, hoping that he would understand every word. None of it worked. As soon as I saw him edge out slightly, he'd spot me and dart back under again.

'He's fast, isn't he?' commented Chris as he walked downstairs after yet another failed attempt to retrieve Morse. 'That's quite the disappearing act he's perfected there.'

Chris was right. My arms were aching for a good old cuddle with this cat, but he was making me wait. Suddenly, it came to me, 'Chris!' I shouted. 'That's what we'll call him; that's what his name should be – Casper the disappearing ghost!' I crouched down on the floor for the last time that night and peered into the big eyes shining out at me.

'Hello, Casper,' I whispered gently, 'welcome home.'

CHAPTER 2

Finding Mum

Casper

Humans like to be in charge. They like to think that they decide things, that they determine what will happen and when. I find this most amusing, as any cat knows it is us who has them under our paws. As I'm very fond of people, I'll give them the benefit of the doubt and see their need for control as one of their many little foibles.

When Sue and Chris came to the house where I lived on that day in December 2002, I wasn't sure, at first, whether I would choose them. They, in turn, thought they had complete freedom to pick whoever took their fancy when choosing 'their' cat. How funny that humans think that way!

The place where I lived was comfortable and safe. It was a large building with plenty of space for me and my fellow cats, and we all got along well. There were lots of us and we stayed downstairs while the human kept to the top part of the house, where there was nothing of interest. The lady who thought she was in charge did have some strange ways.

Despite the size of the house, and the availability of rooms, she chose to feed us from far too few bowls. She expected four of us to share each one! As we obviously couldn't go into the cupboard to get more, we were gracious enough to accept this arrangement. However, I think it indicates the curious nature of some human behaviour. Would you want to share your breakfast, lunch and supper plates with individuals who had been complete strangers not so long before? I didn't think so. Thankfully, cats can be very adaptable - when we want to be.

Humans also have a tendency to talk to us cats constantly. Do you think we can understand your strange warblings, or are you doing it for your own benefit? Whatever the reason, the constant one-sided conversation, which our carer had been having since first light, had brought to our attention that a prospective mum and dad would be arriving today, and that they were called 'Sue' and 'Chris'.

I'd been staying in that house for some time and was quite happy there to begin with. I'd made some good friends, especially with a lovely fellow called Tuppence, and never felt inclined to go home with any of the people who had previously come looking for a feline. However, things change, and I was beginning to hanker after a smaller house where I would have my own bowl and my own bed, and could concentrate on making sure things were exactly as I liked them.

When Sue and Chris arrived, most of the others I shared with ran to have a look. They were keen to make themselves presentable. which is all very well, but as I knew I was naturally friendly and loving (when I chose to be), I didn't see any point in being part of the beauty parade. Instead, I thought I'd be canny, so I watched to see their reaction.

The lady seemed to be the one making the decision, but I was delighted to notice that they were both very kind and caring towards all of my friends. As I listened to their chatter and watched their reactions, I was pleased. These were people I could easily learn to love, but there was a problem: I had grown extremely fond of Tuppence and didn't really want to leave him behind if I chose to move on.

Thankfully, as I looked on, I could see that Tuppence was making a very good impression. They were discussing his looks and temperament, and everything appeared to be going very well. The lady of the house was telling them that Tuppence had a friend - yours truly. At that point, I stood up from my lunch bowl, stretched and began to wash myself.

Now, to be honest with you, washing isn't something I can always be bothered with - no sooner does it seem to be finished than it's time to start again. As a result, I often feel it makes more sense to wait until it absolutely can't be avoided. However, I know that humans put great store in such behaviour on the part of cats (although humans never seem to lick themselves), so I felt it prudent to indulge them.

While I was very keen to make sure I went with Tuppence, I was drawn to Sue when she seemed taken aback by the name I'd been given. For some reason to do with the large black box full of moving pictures that humans stare at for hours on end, I was being referred to as *Morse*. It wasn't a name that suited me terribly well and I was delighted to see that Sue thought so too. That boded well.

Tuppence was placed in one transport container, and one of my friends was unceremoniously removed from the other. I was put in her place, and off we went. I felt I had chosen well.

I was taken to a warm and welcoming house, and my new mum was very careful to ensure that I was as comfortable as could be. Tuppence settled in very quickly, but I was amazed to find that there were as many cats in Sue's place as there had been in my last home - or so it seemed. The smells and sounds of any new accommodation can be frightening, and I needed to make sense of where I was. I hastily beat a retreat upstairs and into the first room I saw.

There was a bed to hide beneath and I determined to stay there until I felt more secure. Both of my new parents were as kind as could be - they brought treats and frequently tried to draw me out, but I would come out only in my own time. If this was the place where I was going live, I needed it to be on my terms.

My mum visited me every hour and did all she could to make me happy. From this I could tell she was indeed a good person, as I had suspected from the start. She brought me some morsels, which were very tempting. All in all, she was teasing me out with her kindness. The ultimate

weapon she had was the one that finally brought me out
from my hiding place. As she called me by my new name,
I knew I was in the place I was meant to be.

Casper ... that was me!

CHAPTER 3

Our Family

Casper may have had a new name, but he wasn't too impressed with his new home. He had come into a house full of other cats, although he wouldn't have known that from his hiding place under the bed. The cats had arrived via different routes and with varied histories. I hoped that Casper would venture out soon so he could meet his new family.

At the time, I was working in a centre for adults with learning disabilities in Weymouth. A few years earlier, one member of staff, Bill, had opened up a cat rescue centre to try to help local kitties. Bill came in one morning to say that they had a geriatric black cat being advertised in the paper the next day. He was hoping to get a good home for him, as he was such an old fluffy darling; he was sure that he would settle well and be a fantastic addition to any carer's life.

My husband Chris is a long-distance lorry driver and was away on a job that day. When he called me later that night, I was full of stories about Bill's cat. No sooner had I finished telling him than he simply said, 'If you want him, Sue, have him.'

I was delighted and skipped into work the next morning to beg Bill, 'Please, please, can we have the cat you were telling me about?'

He laughed at me. 'You could have saved me the money for the newspaper ad if you'd said that yesterday! I'd be over the moon if you took him, and I won't even have to do a house inspection, will I?'

We arranged for Bill to bring him round that night. I already knew what I'd call him – Jack, as in Jack Daniels. At that time, all our cats had 'boozy' names, which makes us sound like a right pair; we're not raving alcoholics, I just liked to have a theme. As always, I was excited waiting for the cat to arrive. Receiving a new member of the family is, to me, as thrilling as waiting for someone to have a baby. Although I'd already chosen the name of this cat, I was still thrilled to find out what he would be like, what his personality would reveal to us and how he would get on with the others.

When Bill brought him in, I was struck by how beautiful this cat was, but as soon as Bill put him down on the carpet, I noticed he had wobbly back legs, which gave him an unusual walk. In fact, he fell over quite often as he walked along. The vet Bill used for the rescue centre said that he had arthritis, but it didn't look like that to me. I'd had cats who'd suffered from the condition and this seemed different.

Jack settled in very well and it wasn't long before we felt as if he had been with us forever. He was good-natured and caused no trouble. Everyone who visited loved him. Like me, they didn't know what to make of his strange walk. I was mystified, until one day a friend called Peter came round for a coffee and saw Jack for the first time.

He watched him for a while, walking around with his distinct wobble, then said, 'That's Edmund.'

'What do you mean?' I asked.

'I know that cat,' Peter said, 'and he's called Edmund.'

I scoffed at him. How could he know my cat?

'Well, there aren't many cats who walk round Weymouth like that, falling over every two minutes, are there?' he replied.

My heart sank. If Peter knew him, then he must belong to someone and wasn't just a stray Bill had picked up. If he belonged to someone, then I'd have to give him back. This was always my concern when taking in cats from rescue centres: perhaps they were lost rather than abandoned, and, if they were found one day, I'd have no choice but to give them back. I would never knowingly keep a cat from its rightful owners, no matter how much I cared for it. I said as much to Peter, who immediately put my mind at rest.

'No, Sue, you've got no worries in that department. I'm thrilled to bits that you've got him. He belonged to this couple I knew – George and Hilary. Their marriage was rocky from the day it started and it didn't get any better. Poor Edmund, or Jack, was a casualty of their divorce, really.'

Peter told me that when Hilary left, George felt he couldn't look after the cat as well, which is why he ended up in the rescue centre. Hilary was now living in the area again, and Peter was able to get in touch with her to say that we had Edmund/Jack. If she wanted him back and could offer him a safe home, I'd have to let him go.

My heart was in my mouth as I waited to hear from Peter. He said he would do all he could to contact Hilary quickly, but as the days passed I got myself into a terrible state, wondering each morning whether it would be my last one with Jack.

Finally, Peter did get back in touch. He had told Hilary that Chris and I had her cat, and explained to her that we loved him dearly. It transpired that she was over the moon at the news: she had been worried about the cat for ages and was now more than happy for us to keep him, as she wasn't in a position to take him back. I felt like jumping up and down when I realized that Jack would be staying with us. Peter gave Hilary regular updates on how he was getting on, and it was a happy ending for everyone.

Jack soon settled in and turned into a very loving boy whose favourite hobby was being brushed; I was quite happy to be the one doing all the brushing. Towards the end of his days, he became unwell, and I tried to treat him as I would want to be treated myself. I'd lie on the floor with him, saying his name over and over again, telling him that everything would be all right and that we loved him. Of course, these were empty words to some degree – the love was there, but he was clearly so ill that everything was *not* going to be all right. I feel that we offer such words of comfort for the peace they may bring through their tone and repetition as much as anything else. I tried to keep my voice steady and my presence calming while I lay beside him. After a while, he would seem calmer. I would whisper to Jack he was such a good boy and I was very proud of him, but I knew that his time was running out. By the time Jack was put to sleep, I'd seen him through so many bad times that I could take some comfort that he was finally at peace.

When we first got Casper, Jack was very much part of the family. He had fit in easily, unlike the new boy. Those early days showed us just how stubborn Casper could be. His determination could outlast everyone else's.

Casper was also sharing his new home with our lovely ginger boy, Oscar. We hadn't chosen Oscar; he'd decided to come and live with us. When we lived in a different house in Weymouth, he'd been homed a few doors down the road from us. It wasn't long after we moved in that he decided he would take up residence too. I've heard lots of similar stories and it seems as if the determined nature of some cats simply won't yield to humans trying to tell them where to live. Of course, if there is cruelty or ill treatment involved, then you can understand why a cat with the freedom to roam would choose a kinder habitat. As far as I could tell, Oscar had a perfectly decent home; he just opted for a change.

I knew one lady who had looked after her cat beautifully for years, then, after a new family moved in next door, she never spent another night with him. He would sit in their garden or on their wall, looking at her as if he could almost remember who she was but didn't really have that much interest. She had done so much for that cat, but he preferred the new people. They were terribly apologetic about it, but, as my friend knew that her cat was being well looked after, she had no concerns – even if she was a little offended by his lack of loyalty. She told me it was as if he'd been waiting for his new family all along and had simply been passing the time with her. How funny cats are!

My Oscar was a very affectionate creature, towards both people and other animals, but he sprayed a lot, so I wondered whether he was stressed about something. The frustrating thing is that you can never know what is going on in a cat's head to make it act in a particular way, and you can never find out whether there was something in its past that is still affecting it. If only they could speak!

Casper had other new companions to get used to besides Oscar and Jack. We also had KP and Peanut, who'd originally been my son's cats. When he was widowed at a tragically young age, my son felt overwhelmed. I was happy to help out by taking in this sister pair. One of the reasons my son felt he couldn't cope with the cats was that KP had thyroid problems and required daily medication to help her live a healthy life. She was a quiet, reserved little thing, quite shy – just like her sister, who recently developed the same thyroid condition. KP and Peanut didn't have much to do with Casper for a while, because, as siblings, they had each other. However, as the years went by and we sadly lost KP to ill health, Peanut and Casper got friendlier.

Clyde, a huge gentle giant of a cat, was friendly with everyone. He weighed over a stone, but he was the one other kitty who broke into KP and Peanut's little gang. Clyde's favourite thing was to lie on his back and have his tummy stroked – he would roll over as soon as he saw anyone go near the cat brush, so you felt obliged to give him what he was so clearly desperate for. He also loved having his face washed by other cats, and it was KP who spent most time doing this.

Maybe it was no wonder that Casper took so long to come out of his hiding place; he must have wondered what mad cat world he had come into. Maybe he'd imagined his new home would be quiet, with only him and Tuppence in it. Instead, he had been transplanted somewhere full of cats and he was going to make us wait until he was ready before we were allowed to feel he had well and truly settled in.

Casper was joining a distinguished extended family of rather naughty cats. Whisky came to mind whenever I thought of all the cheeky things we'd witnessed over the years. She hadn't been with us for long before she got up to nonsense. We prepared for Christmas when she was about four months old, setting up a huge real Christmas tree, laden with baubles on its strong branches. One day I went to work as usual, but when I got back I found the tree lying on its side in the sitting room with all the decorations spread on the floor, and what seemed like a million pine needles festooning the place. Sitting beside the tree was a little black ball of fluff looking terribly innocent – Whisky. As I got closer to her, I noticed an odd bulge in her mouth and then saw the green cable stuck between her lips. Our angelic looking little Whisky had a Christmas tree light in her mouth – thank goodness I'd unplugged the lights before going to work. From then on, we've always had artificial Christmas trees, but the cats in our lives have never run short of mischievous things to do.

CHAPTER 4

Sue's Story

I've always loved cats. Often upsetting events in people's lives can make their bond with other creatures even stronger, and I had one particularly sad experience that I believe strengthened the close ties I felt with animals.

When I was a little girl, I lived in the Middle East, as my father worked as an electrical engineer in an oil refinery. Lots of British workers went there during the 1940s and 1950s. Dad set off to make a life for us when I was five. It was company policy for the men to settle for a few years before they went through the expense and upheaval of bringing the families out too, so I stayed in Britain with my mum and younger sister, Lesley.

However, while Dad was away, Lesley developed cancer. At the time, I was only aware that she was ill and my mum was very upset. Children in those days weren't given much information about things that weren't considered to be their business; perhaps this was a way of protecting us. Whatever the reason,

Lesley's illness had repercussions for all of us. As well as the huge emotional impact of her eventual death, there were practical implications too. The company my dad worked for relaxed their usual regulations and we were allowed to join him quicker than would normally have been allowed.

I was eight by then. Although for a while I thought I had emerged relatively unscathed from losing Lesley, I know now that wasn't the case. At the time, I had no other siblings. Whatever happens in your childhood does have a lasting impact. My early years were affected by Lesley's terrible pain and tragic death, by my father's absence and by the fact that my mother's time was spent caring for Lesley and trying to hold everything together on her own under the most difficult of circumstances.

After Lesley died, there was a sense that we were starting afresh, so my mum and I packed up and prepared to leave the UK. There was some continuity though. When we moved to Bahrain, we took our cat, Blackie, with us. He was really my mum's cat, and I recall her pouring out her heart and soul to him all through Lesley's illness. I remember him very well. I used to take him into my bedroom for cuddles, but he always listened for my mum and ran to her if she called him. I realized from that early age that animals do have a sixth sense for giving what they can to whoever needs them for whatever reason.

I also saw how good Blackie was with Lesley. She was very ill just before she died, and the cat seemed to sense that, staying with her throughout and always being there whenever she could weakly manage to reach out to stroke him. I saw at first hand the connection a person could have with an animal. My mum really depended on Blackie – for some semblance of normality, I guess. Perhaps I see more with maturity, but even as a child I knew there could be something special and I carried that with me. My mum has been dead for a few years now, and I've had children (and grandchildren) myself, but the experiences of those early years have stayed with me and the impact Blackie made was strong.

When we moved to Awali, a municipality within the kingdom of Bahrain, it was to a sort of encampment with fencing that was ten feet high to keep the wild dogs out. There were lots of other families, mainly American, British and Australian, and I was never short of other children to play with. The heat was terribly dry and it took weeks to get used to it, but once that happened, it was perfectly normal to see gangs of dozens of children playing cowboys and Indians in temperatures of over 100 degrees fahrenheit.

It was a strange time, although perhaps I didn't realize it then. My dad took it upon himself to provide us with a lawn, despite the fact that we were living in the middle of the desert. Every day he would drive down to the beach and bring back a few clumps of grass. Of course, it was beach grass, not the lush green meadow type of covering we're used to in England. He would carefully dig little holes in our garden, plug in the beach grass and water it diligently. Each day he would bring back more, and each day he would claim that his 'lawn' was closer to completion. The odd thing was he did eventually manage to create something that resembled a lawn, and everyone referred to it as such.

When I first went to Awali, I attended a school run by Americans, but education there stopped at eleven years of age. Looking back on it, it seems remarkable that I wasn't privy to any of the discussions relating to me. Almost without any warning, it was announced that I would be returning to Britain alone to continue my education at boarding school in Guildford. It was a huge shock. My sister was dead, my mum was still grieving and I had three new siblings I barely knew. Now I was being shipped back to a country that, for me, was associated with illness and grief. My paternal grandparents were there to take care of me during holidays but I was still incredibly lonely in the knowledge that the rest of my family were thousands of miles away and I was expected to be a grown up.

There were a couple of occasions when I went back to Awali for the long summer holiday, but it was very expensive; the fact that I went so rarely suggests that my parents felt it cost too much to have me with them when they were paying so much for my education.

I recall one time flying out on my own from London Airport, as it was then called, on a huge BOAC plane. For some reason, my photograph was in the newspaper, and it looks bizarre to me now, as I was still wearing my school uniform. All I remember about that trip is getting off at Rome for refuelling and going to the bathroom, where I found a tiny little grey and white kitten. I lay on the floor of a half-built toilet in a strange country in all the dust and dirt, and played with the little scrap of a thing until it finally occurred to me that the reason I could hear someone calling my name over and over again was because the lady on the Tannoy was frantically shouting that the plane was waiting for one last passenger and *could I please go there IMMEDIATELY!*

I felt terribly lonely. My grandparents, who were Dutch, did all they could to give me a normal home life during holidays, and they were lovely people, but I longed for the day when I would be part of a family again – a family that had cats at the heart of it.

I made it through boarding school without being terribly academic and ended up with a job in a travel agency. It wasn't as glamorous as I'd hoped; I'd had visions of spending my days organizing exotic trips for people, whereas the reality was that I made cups of tea in the back for everyone else. I soon left that job and got another in Walton-on-Thames, where I was a window dresser in a ladies' gown shop. I loved that position until a chap who worked across the road took notice of me. I managed to ignore him until he got his friends to join in. Suddenly, the naive and embarrassed teenager in me realized that all the mannequins were naked and I was standing in the middle of them. I wished the ground would swallow me up, but I ended up marrying the ringleader instead.

I had been through a lot by then, but I had a vision of how married life would be. I vowed to be the best wife and mother possible, and had a romantic dream of perfect children, a pretty house and, of course, a cuddly kitten to round it all off. I'd spent many happy hours dreaming how idyllic it would be, and animals played a central role in my dream. Sadly, it wasn't to be. The marriage was never right, but as I'm blessed with three wonderful children from those years, I'd never complain. When my husband and I finally separated, I realized that it was time for me to make the world what I wanted to make of it and fulfil my dreams of family life some other way.

CHAPTER 5

Love in Unlikely Places

I was divorced in 1975, two years after my separation. In the meantime, I'd wasted no time in getting a cat. The first one was called Snowy – unsurprisingly, he was a striking white cat. I wouldn't say that he was pretty to begin with, and he certainly wasn't affectionate. Snowy tore all over the place like a mad thing and liked nothing better than to go to the toilet in my rubber plant. He was very destructive, but the plant survived – so much so that I was constantly cutting it back, which meant I had to forgive him. Maybe cats are better gardeners than we give them credit for. After I had Snowy neutered, he calmed down a bit and became very loving. He also turned into a very beautiful cat once he was fed regularly and well.

One day when my daughter Kim was very young, she decided to paint him rainbow colours with her magic markers. I didn't know whether it was dangerous or not, so, somewhat embarrassed, I took the poor cat to the (rather amused) vet, who told me to let it fade away. It didn't seem to bother Snowy in the slightest when Kim began dressing him up in her doll's clothes. He had a lovely nature by this time and never retaliated.

Since then I've heard worse tales of cats having make-up put on them and one little girl even tried to use her mum's hair straighteners on her cat (thankfully, she hadn't worked out how to switch them on), so maybe Kim wasn't too naughty. I do worry about the things children try to do to their pets, but many cats don't even bother to run away; for some reason they lie there letting things be done to them.

I was trying to build a life for us, but it was challenging. I was working full time as an auxiliary nurse in a local hospital, which, thankfully, had a crèche for Kim. I remember it cost me 36p an hour, which took a massive chunk out of my wages. Anyone reading this needs to remember than 36p then was worth a lot more than it is today, and it was a real financial consideration for me, even if it is only the price of a packet of crisps these days. I was happy working there for two years and I learned a huge amount, not only about the job but also about myself.

My next job was as a ward clerk on a GP ward in town, which I enjoyed so much that I stuck with it for thirteen years. The ward was run by a matron – the traditional type that has long gone out of fashion. She imposed lots of rules and regulations, as well as incredibly high standards about attitude and hygiene. We may have had our gripes about her back then, but she was a wonderful woman.

If those sorts of no-nonsense ladies were in charge of NHS hospitals today, I'd wager the infection rates would go down overnight. The sight of nurses wandering around on the streets in their uniforms and then going back onto wards in the same clothes would have made her scream. There are many changes in healthcare that I believe have not been for the good, and the loss of matrons – dragons though they may have been – is one of them. Many of the things she taught me I still remember and apply.

My working life was going well. The children were at school and Kim no longer screamed every time I went off to work. When the children were older and things were more settled, I met someone. Chris was not only fantastic with the kids, but he also accepted me the way I was. I soon realized that some of the aspects of his character that I complained about were his good points, not his bad ones. When he came round, he would get the children out of their beds, mess about with them and get them into such high spirits that it took me hours to get them settled again. What I eventually realized was that he was giving them such happiness that I would have to pay the price – hyper children at midnight. He was fantastic with all three, and that was one of the things that really warmed me to him.

His kindness was not of the 'show-off' variety – it was genuine and heartfelt. One night when I was feeling rather down, he told me to pop round to his flat to tell him all my complaints, which were nothing particularly interesting but seemed vitally important to me at the time. He persuaded me to have a drink or two, and by the time I left, I was much more unsteady on my feet than when I arrived. It was years later that I discovered Chris had followed me home that night to ensure that I got back safely. He stayed a good bit behind me, never drawing attention to himself, and went back to his flat after he'd seen me get myself safely indoors. That sort of kindness is typical of him. When I finally realized how good a man he was, I agreed to marry him.

We wed just before I turned forty. My main demand when Chris proposed was: love me, love my cats. He said that he wasn't a cat person, but, unlike my first husband, he was such a warm and giving person that he was more than happy to try. It took very little time for him to be converted and we've opened our home to a whole menagerie of felines since then. He is just as indulgent and emotional about every one of them as I am.

The three children and I moved in with Chris after the wedding, but one family member wasn't so keen – Snowy. He kept going back to my old house. Chris would patiently trek back for him time after time until we realized that we would have to lock him in until he got the message that this was his new home. Chris became fond of him very quickly, so when I suggested that we get another cat, he was completely supportive.

It was with lightness in my heart that I contacted the cat rescue centre to find the next addition to our family. They did a home visit to ensure that we were suitable for a rescue cat and then suggested I come along the next day to look at the cats they had. I could hardly sleep that night, I was so excited at the thought that I was starting to build the family I'd always wanted.

As soon as I walked in to the rescue centre, I was drawn to a tiny, very slim little girl whom we named Ginny, continuing the theme of cats with drink-related names (Snowy's full moniker was Snowball). She was a beautiful but shy thing of only ten months. She was so dainty – a black and white cat, with four white paws and a white flash on her chest – and very nervous. Ginny had been separated from her brother after a marriage break-up, but this trauma didn't upset her for long. In fact, she became a bossy and domineering creature, who turned out to be a real mummy's girl.

Once she was integrated into her new environment, she made great friends with Snowy, our big fluffy male, who had been living with us for ten years by then (he was back to his original colour after Kim's colouring attempts years earlier had finally worn off). The relationship that developed between Ginny and Snowy was lovely to watch. They were so different in size and temperament, but Snowy always seemed protective and aware of what she needed.

Ginny had her idiosyncrasies just like the other cats I've had. She'd be walking along the pavement quite happily, then she'd suddenly fall off the edge of the kerb. I felt this had to do with her balance rather than any abuse she'd suffered. Oddly, it never seemed to bother her; she treated it as part of life. She was rather like a drunk person who doesn't see anything particularly odd in falling down and simply gets up and carries on. I didn't worry about this aspect of Ginny's behaviour, as the vet said it appeared to cause her no concern and she was just a wobbly little thing.

We were lucky to have Ginny with us for a long time. She was a grand old lady of twenty when she died, and she was one of the cats we had when Casper came into our lives. They couldn't have been more different when it came to settling in. While Ginny had been relatively easy, Casper refused to come out from under that bed.

Of course, Casper didn't stay under the bed forever but he was stubborn. In fact, I think that was the root of the whole problem. He wasn't scared; he wasn't unsure of his new territory; he was just a bit miffed that he had been uprooted from his home of ten months and brought somewhere new.

Chris and I tried everything, but that cat was downright sulky. 'Maybe he wants to go back?' I said to Chris one day.

'Don't be daft,' he replied. 'He's landed on his feet with you. He'll come round – or at least his stomach will get him out of there eventually.'

He was right, and the lure of turkey roll finally proved too much to resist – it was always Casper's downfall. He would be determined to stay outside, set on his travels, but as soon as I dangled a bit of his favourite treat in front of his nose, he couldn't help himself and rushed back in.

When he did deign to come out from under the bed, he settled in very well. After a few exploratory peeks and sniffs, he investigated the whole house. He had his own ways. We soon discovered Casper was a bit of a loner. The only one he would mess about with was Tuppence. They'd chase each other up and down the stairs time after time – it sounded like a herd of elephants. It would go on for hours, then, all of a sudden, Casper would get fed up with Tuppence being so boisterous and give him a nip.

The house was big enough for the cats to have their own space but, even so, I noticed that they tended to gravitate towards each other at naptime – apart from Casper. He would sometimes lie on the same bed or sofa as the others, but always a few feet away, never cuddled up with them. He was a little stand-offish with the other cats, which made sense once we realized how much he enjoyed being with people and how far he'd travel each day to make sure he had contact with as many humans as possible.

Usually one of the ways that new cats coming into the house ingratiate themselves with the already established inhabitants is to clean them as much as possible. I've seen this happen so many times. Cats undoubtedly use grooming as a way of making social connections. Sometimes those who have come from rescue centres will spend hours lavishing attention on the cats who have cemented their place in the household. Casper was never part of this – he never cleaned others and they never cleaned him. In fact, he was often a dirty little devil. One day he would go all out washing himself and his white patches would be lovely, sparkling in the light, then he would go for ages without licking a single bit.

'What a filthy thing you are, Casper,' I'd scold. On more than one occasion I said to Chris that our new arrival was a typical boy who couldn't be bothered having a good scrub until it became absolutely unavoidable.

'Look at the state of you!' I'd chide. 'Your white bits are yellow, and your feet are black! Do you want me to give you a bath?' He'd stare back at me, and I could almost hear him thinking, '*Just you dare*'. On the few occasions I did take a cloth to him, I was shredded to bits and came to the conclusion that I'd leave him to his own devices. He was a very determined creature in so many ways. This became even more apparent as the days turned into weeks and then months.

Tuppence was the exact opposite. In fact, he washed himself so much, he licked patches of his fur away. When we had KP and Peanut, the sisters, Peanut used to spend all day washing the other cats. She'd travel the whole room and I'd watch some of them following little Peanut with their eyes, waiting for their turn, knowing what a dedicated job she'd do.

Gradually, Casper came into his own. He hid under the bed less and less, but I still kept him and Tuppence indoors. Tuppence had been in the rescue home for two months and Casper for ten, so I didn't want them to go outside until they fully realized that this was their home and the place they needed to return to when they did escape. I closed off the cat flap and placed litter trays around, but Casper was dead set on getting out – another way in which he showed his determined nature. Eventually, I had to let them out, as Casper in particular was making such a fuss. He never had a proper miaow, just a pathetic little squeak, and I started to melt a bit too easily when he sat at the front door making that sound to get out.

One of our older cats, Clyde, had a bad back, so I'd constructed a ladder for him to manoeuvre his way around. The garden was on different levels, almost sunken in places, and I'd put a plank from the ground to the top of the fence, with lots of smaller pieces of wood going across it. Everyone else would copy Clyde in order to climb up and walk around the walls.

It wasn't long before Casper started to disappear. He'd hop up on the wooden planks and skip over into other gardens. I generally tried to get him home after a couple of hours, but he would only come in his own sweet time. I tried not to worry about him, but he was the wanderer of the gang. My anxiety lessened, as I assumed that he was investigating gardens nearby. Then one day, about six months after we first brought Casper home, I got a phone call that enlightened me about the sort of cat we'd brought into our lives.

CHAPTER 6

Casper Finds His Paws

Casper started to go out quite a lot. He changed from being the scared little cat hiding under the bed into a very confident fellow who knew his own mind. I often wondered what was going through that mind, as he frequently seemed to have his own agenda. When we first brought him home, I would never have guessed that he would become so determined to go out on his own terms whenever he felt like it. I always worried about my cats, so I tried to keep them inside whenever possible, but Casper was having none of it.

Once he'd settled with us, he broke a number of windows and even attacked nailed down cat flaps in his desire not to be an indoors puss. I made sure he had a disc attached to his collar with his name and my number on it for when he did wander, in case he got lost or something happened to him. I was beginning to think that my initial assessment of him had been spot on: he wasn't shy or scared when he first came to us; he was stubborn. More of his stubborn streak was being revealed practically every day.

One afternoon, the phone rang as I got back from a shift at work. As soon as a woman asked, 'Have you got a cat called Casper?' my heart sank.

I hadn't seen him that morning before I left and my immediate response came from the heart. 'Oh my God – he's dead, isn't he?'

She laughed kindly. 'No, he's fine – actually, he's in my work car park.'

I asked where that was and was shocked when she said the offices were over a mile and a half away. How on earth had he got there? The possibilities were endless and I had to assume that most likely he'd walked, or maybe he got into someone's car and popped out when they arrived at work.

As I didn't drive, I caught the bus to the car park with a basket in my hand. When I picked Casper up, I felt the same mix of emotions that he would inspire in me throughout his many adventurous years: relief that he was safe and anger that he could have been in danger. 'You are a naughty boy, Cassie. Why do you have to get me so worried? Why can't you just stay at home rather than wander around?'

I couldn't be cross at him for long as I was so pleased he was coming home again. Although when I realized that the bus had long gone and I would have to walk the full distance after a tiring day at work, carrying a wriggling cat in an uncomfortable wicker basket, I probably did have a few more comments!

Casper's escapade decided my next course of action: he would have to get chipped. If he had an accident or got lost, then at least I would stand a chance of getting him back again if a vet could scan him and get my details from the national database. I made the appointment for the very next day.

In the morning, I gave him a talking to as I got myself ready. 'Right,' I said. 'This is for your own good. You're a bit of a wanderer, aren't you?' He looked up at me as if he understood every word. 'Well, it looks like I can't do much about that, but I can make sure that you can find your way back to me if you ever get lost.' My tone softened as I gazed at this cat I already loved so much. 'Oh, Casper, please try to stay close to home. I don't want to lose you.'

I took Casper into the surgery and plopped him down on the table to have him scanned. 'He's chipped already,' said the vet.

'What?' I shrieked. I hadn't expected that and would have thought the cat rescue people would have given me that information when I took him home.

The vet asked me what I was going to do, but it seemed quite clear to me: Casper wasn't my cat. There was somebody out there, distraught that their cat had been missing for some time, possibly assuming that he was dead. 'I have to find out who he's registered to,' I said. 'And I'll have to give him back, won't I?'

I went home with a heavy heart. Casper scooted out of his basket and went upstairs without a care in the world, as I threw myself down on the sofa and wondered what I would do without him. He had already become such a big part of our lives that I couldn't bear to think about giving him up. It would undoubtedly be the right thing to do and I just had to focus on that.

I rang Cats Protection as soon as I felt able to. After I'd told them what had happened and given them the registration number the vet had found, the woman from Cats Protection called the company that keeps all the details. The time passed very slowly as I waited to hear what they'd learned. Within thirty minutes, she rang me back with a request that delighted me, but which perplexes me to this day. 'Sue, please keep him,' she pleaded. 'There's no way he can go back to the place he came from; it would be heartbreaking. Please, will you let him stay with you?'

Of course this was what I'd wanted all along. I loved Casper dearly, but what was going on? All I could get from her was that he'd been living in a terrible environment and Cats Protection couldn't allow him to go back there. I got the impression that Casper had escaped from whatever horrible life he'd led and lived rough for a while before being taken to the rescue centre by some kind person ten months before I re-homed him.

I was delighted by the news that Casper would officially be mine. The Cats Protection lady said that the details on the chip records would be changed immediately to reflect the change in ownership. From that point, I felt that Casper was genuinely mine, but I often wondered what sort of life he must have had.

As time went on, we found out more about him: how he seemed unafraid of traffic, how much he loved cars and lorries and how dogs left him totally unfazed. I picked up a few other hints from the cat rescue lady, and when I pieced it all together, the most likely scenario seemed to be that he had lived with a travelling community. By saying this, I'm not casting aspersions on people who choose that lifestyle, but if Casper had been moved from pillar to post, then it wouldn't have been the best environment for him, but it would explain why he had no fear of other animals and why he was drawn to vehicles. Still, as with so many of my cats, I would never know the full story. I would simply have to ensure that while he was with me I gave him – and them – the best life possible and didn't dwell on the past.

I wondered where Casper went. There would be days when he stayed nearby and would come as soon as I called – or when he got a whiff of turkey roll – but there were other times when he wouldn't come back for hours no matter how long or how loudly I called his name. He had such wanderlust.

He had little fear of dogs, which worried me, as I thought he might meet his match one day. He would lie in the grass wherever we lived and never flinch when dogs went past. In fact, one summer, a neighbour had a lovely little spaniel puppy she used to walk at the same time every day. The puppy would strain at the leash every time it got to our garden path, where Casper lay idly watching the world go by. I think he was desperate to play, even with a cat, but Casper never flinched and never raised his hackles. He looked at the puppy as if he were just another pedestrian going about his business.

Some time after we got Cassie, we moved to Frome in Somerset. I always worried when we changed location, as it can take cats a while to get their bearings. I tried to keep them indoors until they realized they were in a new home and they had some idea of the new smells and sounds around them. The old cottage we bought had a huge stone wall around it, which Casper couldn't get over by himself. Every time he managed to sneak out, he would have a jolly good try at scaling it, even though it was impossible. Eventually he discovered a gate, which, though closed and locked, he could squeeze around. On the other side of the wall was a car park linked to the local doctor's surgery, and I worried that he was hanging around cars again. However, it was clear that it would take a greater force than me to keep this cat indoors, so I had no option but to let him wander every now and again.

I'd discovered by this stage that I was suffering from some quite severe health problems and I needed heart surgery. Before that could happen, I had to get my blood pressure down, so I was visiting my GP quite a lot. One day I arrived for my appointment and checked in at reception. I was directed to the waiting area as usual, and as I walked towards a chair, I couldn't believe my eyes when I saw Casper.

He was sitting, bold as brass, on one of the plastic seats, as if it were the most natural thing in the world. I had an early morning appointment and no one else was there yet – thankfully. 'Casper!' I whispered sharply. 'What on earth are you doing here?' He gave me a lazy look, as if he couldn't be bothered to explain himself, then settled back down again. I looked around quickly, expecting to see a receptionist bearing down on me with demands to get Casper out immediately, but the room remained empty. I gathered him up in my arms, all the while telling him what a naughty boy he was, and took him into the car park, shooing him in the direction of the cottage.

When I was called in to see the doctor, I was surprised that my blood pressure wasn't through the roof. All I could think was that Casper had trotted into the surgery before me and had hopped onto a chair while I was talking to the receptionist. I felt very relieved that they hadn't spotted him on this one-off occasion when he had been so cheeky.

The next week I was back at the practice for more tests and I was running a little late. When I got there, I was told to go straight through. There were a number of doctors on duty, all with offices attached to each other. As I sat there with the blood pressure cuff around my arm, discussing the results of my previous tests, I almost fainted when I heard someone in another room shout, 'Get that cat out of here! This is a surgery not a pet shop!'

I knew it was Casper. After all, how many other cats were likely to be doing exactly the same thing he had done? I couldn't jump up and say that I was off to get my cat, so I got through my appointment as quickly as possible and hurried home, only to find Casper innocently waiting for me on the doorstep.

After I had seen Cassie a few more times at the practice, it became clear that, despite the doctors being less than happy when he followed patients in for their consultations, the staff were well aware of his presence and were relaxed about him being there.

One day I gathered up the courage to raise the issue with a receptionist when I was making my next appointment. 'Erm . . .' I began, hesitatingly, 'do you know there's sometimes a cat in here?'

She smiled as if it was the most natural thing in the world. 'Yes, yes, we do,' she said. 'Isn't he lovely?'

I couldn't argue with that. 'Well, actually, I think he's mine,' I admitted.

'Is he? Is Casper yours?'

We had a little chat and she told me that he was in quite often, that they had got his name from his disk and that, as long as he kept out of the doctors' rooms, they were all generally happy to have him there. This astounded me – how kind and how eccentric at the same time. Only in Britain would a strange, wandering cat be seen as a normal addition to a healthcare practice. My heart lifted at the thought of how kind these people had been to Casper while I had been living in blissful ignorance.

The receptionist told me there were lots of patients who'd commented on how nice it was to see Casper; when they came in stressed or worried, he managed to distract them for a little while. The more I thought about it, the more I felt this was probably why he was so welcome.

I'd heard of programmes that took animals into hospitals to help long-term patients, as they can help lower blood pressure, reduce stress and release 'happy hormones'. In fact, at the world-renowned Great Ormond Street Hospital, there is a pet therapy project that brings animals in on a regular basis. The hospital has visits from guinea pigs, kittens, dogs and even once a Shetland pony. The medical staff has found that young patients feel much more relaxed and comfortable, even in such a difficult environment, when furry friends are around. Across the country there are thousands of pet therapy dogs and cats who've done amazing work, and I felt, in his own small way, that Casper was achieving something similar. The irony was that while he may have been helping the blood pressure of other people, his escapades and travels were making mine worse!

What was amazing about Casper was that he expected to be allowed to go anywhere he wanted. He never seemed to show nervousness about walking into any place that took his fancy, despite many of them being less than cat friendly. I didn't expect him to read the signs for the surgery or whatever, but surely most cats would have been put off by strange buildings full of people they didn't know? Not Casper. Perhaps he saw the stickers saying that no dogs were allowed and took that to mean that cats were more than welcome.

Casper had a certainty about him that made people accept him. If he was sitting on a chair in a doctor's waiting room, then perhaps that was where he was meant to be. It was as if he could persuade people to give him what he wanted just by being there. He was a calm cat who never bothered humans. He liked their company but waited for them to approach him a lot of the time. He wasn't one of those cats who constantly pushed and rubbed for attention; maybe if he had been, he would have been less welcome. As it was, he followed people into their appointments and trotted about quite freely, but never in a way that suggested anything other than that he was a cat going about his business. He was becoming well known, and finding his feet (or paws) around town, but I had no idea just how popular he was.

CHAPTER 7

A Comfortable Life

I usually went into town to collect prescriptions from the doctor but, as I had to take quite a lot of time off work in preparation for my heart surgery, I needed to find somewhere closer to home. There was a pharmacy attached to the health centre so beloved by Casper. It was used by patients and general customers alike, and I decided to start going there for my medication. One day I popped in after I'd been to the GP. I hadn't seen Casper next door and wondered where he was. Imagine my surprise when I saw him on a chair in the chemist's as if he were waiting for his own pills and potions.

The shop had a counter where the pharmacist got prescriptions ready and there were two seats for people to wait while they were being prepared. On one of these sat Cassie, large as life, as if he belonged there. 'That's my cat!' I squealed to the woman at the cash desk. 'How often is he in here?'

She laughed at me. 'How often? Well, let's put it this way,' she said, 'we used to have one seat where people would wait for their prescriptions – now we have two! We had to get him one of his own, as he was here so often that no one else could sit down.'

Casper's escapades were getting more and more outlandish. What was remarkable was that everyone was falling in line with what he wanted. Just like the staff at the doctor's surgery, all of those who worked in the chemist's shop seemed friendly and accepting of Casper. They knew his name – they'd checked his tag too – and thought nothing of the funny little cat who often sat there from nine in the morning until he was kicked out at closing time. I recalled the number of days I'd been tearing my hair out, fearful for Casper outdoors, roaming the streets in all weathers, when, in actual fact, he was warm and dry, sitting on a chair specially provided for him. I rushed home to get my camera and took some photos of him. He looked like royalty waiting for his servants to fulfil his every need – which was pretty much how it was.

I was told that there were a lot of elderly ladies who used that pharmacy and they had all adopted Casper. Some of them used to pick him up from his seat while they waited for their prescriptions. They'd wander around the shop, carrying him like a baby on his back in their arms, and giving him lots of cuddles. One of the shop assistants told me he was giving people so much comfort by being there and providing something for them to look forward to when they had little else in their lives. He wasn't being entirely altruistic though, as, according to the assistants, my Casper lapped it all up and was getting plenty of love from lots of people.

'He's such a handsome boy, isn't he?' one of them commented.

I had to bite my tongue to prevent myself from replying, 'Yes, when he's clean!' I didn't want to draw attention to the fact that he wasn't always the most hygienic of cats in case it gave them a reason to stop his little visits.

The way Casper was treated by the staff in both the GP's surgery and the chemist's shop displays what I feel is a wonderful but sometimes eccentric British tendency to love animals – sometimes we have more time for them than we do for our fellow humans. The British public is certainly very generous when it comes to supporting animal charities: according to the Charities Aid Foundation figures, the NSPCC receives only £2 million more in donations than the RSPCA; the Dogs Trust receives around £34 million in donations every year and Cats Protection around £27 million.

While many outsiders may view Britain as a country overly keen on bureaucracy and rules, it seems that we often bend them beyond the call of duty when animals are concerned. The Queen herself is forever associated with her love of corgis, and many have heard the story of Mrs Chippy, the tabby cat who sailed from London on *Endurance* with Sir Ernest Shackleton. Major British institutions have a history not merely of housing but of positively encouraging feline companions.

Only a few years ago, details were revealed under the Freedom of Information Act about the cats that the Home Office had been keeping at its London headquarters since 1883. Originally, cats were introduced to deal with the natural problem of mice in an old building, but, in 1929, the status of the cat was formally recognized when one penny a day was paid from the official accounts for food. All the Home Office cats were black and all were called Peter. When the Home Office began to set up satellite establishments across the country, each put in an official request for their own 'Peter'.

In the late 1950s, whichever Peter was in residence in the London Home Office was *cat*apulted to fame when he appeared in a documentary. When well-wishers offered gifts of tasty titbits and snacks in celebration of his work, they were told that this was against the rules that prevent civil servants from accepting gifts. After the death of that Peter, the Isle of Man offered one of their famous Manx cats to replace him. The fact that she was a girl could have jeopardized the line of 'Peters', which had become a tradition by then, but the civil servants got round it by calling her 'Peta.'

Nor was Downing Street, the heart of British government, immune to the attractions of a pet. Wilberforce resided with three Prime Ministers – Edward Heath, Harold Wilson and Margaret Thatcher – thanks to his reputation as a great mouser. By the time he retired in 1987, he'd managed to affect the Iron Lady to the extent that she was reputed to have brought him back a tin of sardines from a state visit to Moscow.

It wasn't long after the death of Wilberforce, soon after his retirement, that a new cat came into office at Number 10. Humphrey, named after a character in *Yes Minister*, wandered into the seat of power one day and simply took up residence. Apparently, he too appealed to the Prime Minister, for his cost of £100 a year was much less than the £4,000 for a pest control officer who'd allegedly never caught a mouse. Humphrey saw the departure of Mrs Thatcher and the arrival of John Major, and even lasted until Tony Blair brought a Labour government to power in 1997. He was given free rein to wander between Numbers 10 and 11 Downing Street and was famous enough to have his own book published. He met Bill Clinton, President of the USA at the time, and perhaps discussed whether Socks, the White House cat, had any special privileges he did not.

Humphrey found himself at the heart of a scandal when it was alleged that he was responsible for the death of a family of baby robins. The Prime Minister quickly jumped to his defence, claiming 'Humphrey is not a serial killer'. It was later suggested that Mr Major knew this categorically, as it was he, not Humphrey, who had disturbed the robins' nest, thus scaring away the parents.

Humphrey survived the slur on his character, but did not manage to last through the residency of Mr

Blair. After only six months, Humphrey disappeared and some journalists suspected foul play. On enquiring what had happened to the Chief Mouser, they were told he had retired due to kidney problems. In the hope of more interesting headlines, questions were asked about whether he had been put to sleep, as it was alleged the Prime Minister's wife was allergic to cats. In a scene worthy of Britain's reputation as eccentric when it comes to animals, a number of select journalists were taken to a secret location to meet Humphrey in his retirement. Many of them knew him of old and could confirm his identity, so a national crisis was averted. To my mind, Humphrey looks rather like Casper and I wonder whether it is just in the nature of fluffy black and white cats to cause trouble?

It was not until Mr Blair was succeeded by Gordon Brown in 2007 that a new cat came to Downing Street. Sybil – again named after a TV character, this time from *Fawlty Towers* – was believed to have come from the new Chancellor Alastair Darling's home in Edinburgh. Sadly, Sybil didn't settle and it was decided that she should return to Scotland. However, before this happened she became very ill and passed on.

I think it is delightful that in the midst of political shenanigans and top-level debates, those in power still have time for furry friends. Perhaps they, too, benefit from the lowered blood pressure and stress levels that come from having animals around – who knows? Whatever the reason, I do hope it continues, and I am proud to think that, in his own small way, Casper played a part in helping people during what may have been very difficult times in their lives.

Dear Cassie – helping all those people without knowing it, certainly without *me* knowing it. It makes me sad to think of old people alone without anyone to tell their worries to, but the thought that Casper gave them some companionship is heart-warming and comforting. There is no doubt that some people feel able to relate to an animal in ways they can't with another person. I hope Casper was there for people when they needed him.

It was Casper's friendliness and love for humans that made him a special cat. In truth, he was an ordinary little cat who was starting to have an extraordinary effect. I used to laugh at his adventures in Frome, but I could never have imagined what would happen once we moved to Plymouth.

CHAPTER 8

How to go Places and Make Friends

Casper

🐾

Obviously, I had a life before I found my mum. When we discovered each other, I was getting on a bit and no longer a little kitten. I was a cat with a past! While she may have been keen to discover what that past entailed, I enjoyed being something of a 'mystery cat' with an eye on the future. In the days before mum I learned to survive and be comfortable around humans, and that's what matters most. I used what I'd learned to make sure life was as nice for me as it could possibly be.

It was about this time that I realized my understanding of the human world was something that could help cats and people alike. Because I'd always been a nomad at heart, I'd built up a lot of knowledge about the skilful ways in which journeys could be undertaken and friends made, which I will share with you now.

Casper's basic rules for filling the day

1 Decide where you want to go.

2 Go there.

3 If there are impediments (and humans must be given some credit for the many ways in which they manage to create obstacle courses out of the most innocent household articles), see this as nothing more than a challenge. Windows and doors always open somehow. It is generally useful to feign sleep until such openings appear, then spring to life and exit, leaving your human too confused to catch you in time.

4 Previous reconnaissance missions may have given you an idea of where to while away a few pleasant hours. If this is the case, head to that source of heat, food or company immediately. If you are undecided, listen for happy human noises, the smell of turkey roll and an absence of barking.

5 I have always found places in which people sit down in large groups are highly conducive to cats. Human vet buildings (or 'GP surgeries' as they like to call them), or places where they wait to buy their flea treatment (they call these buildings 'the chemist' or 'the pharmacy'), usually have comfortable seats placed there for cats. Indeed, if humans also wish to sit down, another

seat will be provided for any feline visitors, which is a
charming kindness and much to their credit.

6 Ignore shouting unless it is accompanied by the throw-
ing of objects or energetic chasing.

7 Always behave as if it is perfectly natural and normal
for you to be in the place of your choice.

8 If your human appears, remain calm. They tend to be
quite surprised that we have lives beyond their homes
and gardens. If they see us beyond those confines, they
get confused and assume that you 'need to go home'. This
is odd: if you 'needed' to get home, you would go home,
so it's best to stay seated, pretend to sleep if needs be or
ignore them if that's best. They'll soon realize you have
a right to be there - as the other humans have already
recognized - and they may even think they've imagined
it all.

9 You will probably receive quite a lot of attention in these
places, which should be accepted (especially if that was
the object in the first place). Prepare to be carried like
a human baby, praised for being 'clever' (this involves
doing nothing more than being yourself) and told many
secrets and worries.

10 Go home as if nothing had ever happened.

CHAPTER 9

Finding More Friends

My affinity with animals is an integral part of me, and my husband Chris accepts that. He never laughs when I stop in the street to move a worm out of harm's way, or if I rant at people on holiday when I see them being thoughtless or cruel to strays. Chris takes it as part of me, and I will always be grateful to him for that. When we married we couldn't imagine the struggles we would face, but I believe that his understanding of me from the start allowed us to build such a strong base as a couple that we rose to the challenges with greater strength when they came.

I enjoy watching the cats grow with each other as much as I love getting to know them myself. What they've taught me about patience and care is immeasurable. No pair did more in that regard than Clyde and a cat called Gemma.

We got Gemma from a couple who'd broken away from the official Cats Protection branch where we lived and set up an independent cat rescue group. I befriended this couple and kept in touch with them even when I wasn't looking to add new kitties to my life. I always enjoyed visiting Ted and Rosemary, so one beautiful summer afternoon I'd cycled over to see them in their cat centre. Chris was going to meet me there when he'd finished work.

When I arrived, Rosemary called out, 'Just have a wander round, Sue, and I'll be with you as soon as I can.' She always had her hands full, attending to all the residents, but I was quite used to spending some time on my own, happily looking at who was there and what they were all up to.

I was pottering around, checking all the pens and making sure that the cats were fine, when this lovely creature came straight up and looked at me in such a strange way. It was almost as if she were looking into my soul – I felt quite spooked. I wasn't in the market for another cat, so I tried to put it out of my mind. Chris and I met up later at the centre and we had a chat with Ted and Rosemary before we headed off. I hadn't realized that, when we visited, he'd also taken to wandering around and looking in all the pens, so when he told me what he'd been up to, I was quite surprised.

When we got home, he kept chatting about all the cats and finally said, 'Did you see the white one with the grey bits on her by any chance?' I knew he was talking about the same little girl who'd stared at me, so I said I had and was shocked when he told me that the same thing had happened to him. 'She stared at me so hard, for so long, that I felt as if I'd known her before,' Chris told me. 'Isn't that funny?' he said. 'I felt a connection there – we just sort of gelled.' It was odd. Chris loved animals by now, but this was the first time I'd heard him talk like that. This little cat had really got to him.

We didn't say anything else about it that night, but as I was dropping off to sleep, Chris whispered to me. 'You know, Sue, that little white and grey cat? If you want her, that's absolutely fine by me.' That was as good as him asking for her.

The next day I called Rosemary and she was delighted that we were going to be Gemma's new carers. She brought her round that very afternoon and told me a little of her story. 'The poor thing has been housed twice already,' she said. 'People take a rescue cat and expect it to come into their lives and settle immediately. It doesn't happen like that – it takes a lot longer than one day.' She told me that Gemma had been housed with a dog and another cat and she was too scared of both of them to fit in instantly, so she'd been brought back almost immediately. The same thing happened the next time: she was given hardly a moment before that family decided she wasn't right for them either.

When Rosemary left, I made a vow that it would be third time lucky for little Gemma now that she was with us. There was no way I was going to dump her again. She eventually came out of her shell, and by the time that had happened, Rosemary had told me a little more of her story. She'd been found in a transport yard, covered in diesel. The men in the yard had tried to do their best for her, by making sure she was fed, but she was a nervous, twitchy thing. They contacted Rosemary, as they were worried about her. There was a suspicion that she had jumped a lorry, as she had no collar or chip, but, really, we knew nothing about her.

Gemma was hard work – even harder than Casper. Settling her took six months. I didn't know much about what had happened in her past but she must have been forced to fend for herself at some point, as she was incredibly defensive with the others, hissing and spitting, especially around food. It was as if she always felt she had to fight for it, and there would never be enough.

As we were her third attempt at re-homing, I felt that we owed it to her to keep trying. The poor thing had been passed from pillar to post, and it would have been unfair to give up on her quickly. However, there was always the worry that the other cats would get overwhelmed and possibly even leave if the attacks went on for too long. Gemma eventually responded to love and care and became the most beautiful cat. With grooming and a little help with her hygiene, it transpired that she was a stunning Maine Coon.

Her main delight was being outside in the warmth – what a sun worshipper that cat was! When I took her to the vet for the first time, I was warned to be very careful and protect her from sun exposure because the white patches she had would make her more susceptible to skin cancer. I got a big floral parasol and propped it up in the garden for her to sit under once we knew her habits. This protected her from the brilliant sunshine, but she sneaked out from under it quite a lot to lie in other patches.

After she had been with us for a while, I noticed she was getting a scab on her ear that I knew hadn't come from a cut. I took her back to the vet and received the sad news that she did, indeed, have skin cancer. He also noticed that she had a sty under her eyelid – this was also cancerous. The vet was absolutely brilliant and performed plastic surgery on her face, but he had to amputate her ear. However, the disease spread and, within a month, Gemma started walking in continuous circles. The vet believed that she was having terrible headaches and this was her way of coping with them.

Gemma still sought out the sun, no matter how tiny the spot. The amazing thing was that Clyde, who was not a sun worshipper, started to sit with her. The more ill she became, the more dedicated he was. Gemma was never alone; she always had her friend beside her. I swear he knew she was poorly and he was trying to offer her some comfort. I had a lump in my throat every time I saw them together: Gemma getting weaker and Clyde diligently keeping watch. When she got up from her spot and started to walk round in circles, he'd wait until she tired herself out and came back to him. It was incredibly humbling to witness such patience and consideration.

As time went on, her walking in circles got worse and I knew the time had come to make a decision. In my heart, I knew she'd have to be put to sleep. I was on my own the day I went, as Chris was working abroad, and I felt such loneliness and sorrow. Every time I've been in this position, I've done it by myself, and it is a great burden to carry. Many people say that animals are lucky: they have us to make the decision for them and help them to cross the rainbow bridge. I appreciate and understand that way of thinking, but it doesn't stop the loss from hurting.

When poor little Gemma was being prepared for her injection, I swear she held out her paw towards me as if to say 'bye bye'. I cried my heart out – as I have done with all of them, and as I'm sure I'll continue to do. All the cats touch me so deeply that I can't help but be affected.

I don't feel guilty about making the choice to help them pass over, but I'm a little sad my decision does, in effect, betray my animals, even when I'm trying to do the right thing by them. Gemma wasn't the first pet I'd had to do this for, and she won't be the last. All I could do as I said goodbye was promise her that I'd never forget her and make a commitment to do all I could for any other cat who crossed my path. It would be my life's work and a privilege.

CHAPTER 10

Keeping Track of Casper

After a while, we moved from Frome to Crewkerne, an old-fashioned market town in Somerset. Unfortunately our new house was on a busy road. I knew for certain that Casper was a wanderer, so I had many worried moments. I didn't know many people to begin with, so I had no idea whether the residents and workers here would be as tolerant of Casper as they had been in our previous location. He was a very trusting cat and I felt he was willing to assume all humans were good. I shuddered to think what might happen if he put his faith in the wrong person, but I kept my fingers crossed that all would remain rose-tinted for my lovely cat.

Casper was obsessed with crossing the road outside our house. I used to say to Chris that I had no idea why, as there was absolutely nothing of interest on the other side. It was as if he had a nosiness gene. I'd sometimes watch him from my window with my heart in my mouth as he narrowly dodged a car. He was behaving the same way he had in Frome: always trying to nip out, always trying to be at the heart of things.

It was bad enough when he ventured out during the day, but when he started disappearing overnight, it was even worse. This was a new development in Casper's wanderlust; perhaps he was just spreading his wings (or paws). His travels had all been so successful in the past maybe he thought it was time to try a few night-time excursions. I never knew if he'd be there in the morning when I came down, though eventually I did manage to piece together a few things to get some idea of where he'd been.

At the bottom of our garden was a building where the sails for HMS *Victory*, Nelson's famous flagship, had originally been made, but it had been converted to a block of offices. One day I got chatting to a lady who worked there. As we talked, I saw Casper boldly trotting down the road to the offices.

'Oh, there's Casper,' she remarked, as my eyes popped open wider.

'How do you know him?' I asked.

'He's always hanging around where I work,' she said. 'He's like our little office mascot.'

Is he, now? I thought to myself.

'We all like to have a little cuddle with him when he pops in, give him a few treats and suchlike. He often hangs around all day and the girls in the office just love having him around.'

Well! It hadn't taken Casper long to return to his old tricks. He may not have found a pharmacy or a doctor's surgery in which to while away the day, but he'd still managed to access attention. This lady told me he was very popular among the office staff and brightened up their day. They looked forward to him coming in as a break from the monotony of their routine. On the days when he found something better to do, there was general disappointment that their little visitor hadn't appeared.

The office block wasn't his only new hangout. There was a family a few doors down the road from me who had actively been encouraging Casper into their cottage. When another neighbour told me about this, I was quite confused – he was clearly someone else's cat, as they could see from his name tag and disc, but perhaps, like me, they couldn't resist any visiting cat even if it had a perfectly good home. I felt it was asking for trouble with this cat in particular though, and it probably contributed to his wanderings. I plucked up the courage to go and speak to them and, lo and behold, when I got there, who should be lying in a basket by the fire but Casper.

The woman who lived there had bought it especially for him, but when I asked her whether she thought he was homeless, she admitted that she knew he lived with me. It felt as if he were a tug-of-love cat and I was going to have to fight for him – my chances were good, as the lady was heavily pregnant. I had to ask her to stop making her home quite so attractive to him. Casper was a clever enough cat but he was bound to be confused with the house move, the new roads and now a complete stranger inviting him in to a nice new bed. I asked her if she could please stop doing this and, if he visited again, to encourage him gently to return to his own house.

He continued to wander, and I suspected that he was still visiting his nice other bed, but I couldn't keep haranguing this woman, who was only being kind. However, there was a lingering feeling, perhaps some sort of sixth sense, that made me concerned about those particular trips.

One day in March 2005, Casper had his breakfast as usual and then went out after about ten minutes. From what I can tell, he then wandered down to the car park beside the office block from where he could often get over the wall into the house and garden of the family who'd bought him his new basket. However, instead of disappearing for the day, he came back within the hour. As I was standing in the kitchen, tidying away the breakfast things, I heard a strange snuffling noise, like hedgehogs make. I opened the back door only to see my darling Casper covered in blood.

His face was almost unrecognizable. All I could do was grab him in my arms and run to the vet. The news was awful but it could have been worse. I was told that he had definitely been hit by a car and, although he had no apparent fractures, his jaw and mouth were both very bruised and he was extremely lucky to be alive. As he was cut and shaking with shock, he had to stay in overnight.

For the rest of his days, Casper's lower lip area always had a black mark where he'd been hit and he dribbled slightly whenever he ate or drank. I had to keep an eye on him in case he developed sores on his lip. I couldn't help but think that he had used up one of his nine lives with this accident. He was very lucky to have got out of it with only a few scrapes. 'Oh, Casper,' I whispered to him one night when he was safely at home, 'you're always going to give me sleepless nights, aren't you? I don't think I'm ever going to be settled with you around, young man.'

I went back to the house that Casper seemed so drawn to and asked the lady once more if she would please stop encouraging him – knowing full well that if Casper was determined, both she and I would have quite a job stopping him from doing whatever he pleased. I was terribly worried by the fact that he had probably been hit trying to get to this house with the comfy new basket, and was so relieved when the woman said that she would keep her door closed to her little visitor and not let him in, even if he turned those pleading eyes on her.

As I suspected, it wasn't long before Casper threw a cat-shaped spanner in the works. Although he must have been very confused to have been given a new bed one day and faced with a closed door the next, he soon found a way round it. I discovered that he climbed onto the slanted roof of the house and got in through the bathroom window, which was always open. It was only when the woman had her baby and found Cassie in the airing cupboard one day that she made serious attempts to keep him out, and he finally got the message.

Casper may have had barred from one of his haunts, but he still had the attention of the women in the office block. Sometimes as I walked past, I would see him on the car park wall, surrounded by admirers, who would all clap him as he lay in the sun. His accident had me worried though, and I printed lots of posters to hand round the local offices, asking people to look out for him and make sure that he wasn't locked in overnight. I also wanted to make sure that everyone knew that he had a loving home, so they weren't tempted to take him away – that was one of my biggest fears, as he was such a friendly cat. The poster read:

PLEASE HELP!
You may have noticed a black and white
cat in the car park or in the offices.
He is called Casper and he is wearing
a collar with two tags on it.
Casper is very friendly and as quick as lightning.
Can I ask you to be vigilant for him and check
that he is not locked in overnight? He comes from
a loving home and we would really appreciate
whatever little you can do to help us keep him safe.
Thank you.

Wherever we've lived, Casper has caused trouble and I've always had to appeal to people's good nature, asking them to be vigilant. Sometimes they have been more than happy to help; on other occasions, as I would later find out, they would take offence and suggest that I was trying to get others to look after my cat, which was never my intention.

Casper didn't have to be out and about to be naughty. I remember one Christmas Day when I thought I'd be terribly prepared and get the food for Boxing Day ready in advance. I took out pork chops and sausages to defrost for the next day's dinner, but I must have been full of Christmas spirit to think for a second Casper wouldn't help himself. I didn't hear a thing, but somehow he managed to knock the top plate off and help himself to a few mouthfuls. All I could think about was that he might get food poisoning, so I quickly cooked all the meat for the cats to have as their Christmas Day treat. I suspect the others put him up to it.

Any time I was frying sausages, he'd appear from nowhere when he heard the sizzle to sit beside me, almost on tenterhooks, looking as if he hadn't been fed for a year. It always worked, and he always got his way. There were other times when Chris was away that I would treat myself to dinner in front of the television. As I sat there paying more attention to what was on the box than what was on my plate, I'd often see a paw reach up, quietly and swiftly, and grab something.

Casper would eat anything that wasn't his. One day, after a long road trip, Chris and his friend Martin decided that they would have fish and chips. We were both in the kitchen, and while Martin popped to the loo,

Casper helped himself. Martin came back to find a cat sitting in the middle of his chips, licking his lips happily.

I wonder whether his need to eat anything, any time, was a product of his past? Maybe he never knew where his next meal was coming from; that's why we indulged him so much. It wasn't just me – whenever Chris came home, he would do so with a package of blue cheese for Casper. We never begrudged him anything and I'd do anything to be able to buy him his little treats again.

Apart from food, Casper's other great love was gadgets – a typical boy! I used to tease him with the DVD remote control. I'd press the button as he sat there staring at the machine, and he would catch the little tray that holds the DVD as it popped out. Just as he got his paw on it, I'd press the button again and slide it in as he sat there with his head to one side, looking confused. He'd sit there for ages, watching as it went in and out, in and out. Sometimes he would realize that the VCR was close by too, so he would give up his reconnaissance mission for a few moments to stick his paw into the videotape slot, then trot back to the DVD player again. Perhaps we should all spend more time getting such pleasure from simple things – it certainly worked for Casper.

CHAPTER 11

Trying to Help, Trying to Love

Like all pet owners, I loved all of Casper's little idio-syncrasies. I've often wondered whether part of the reason for getting more cats is to fill the gap left every time I lose one. Of course, they're all different and can't directly replace each other, but Casper ticked an awful lot of boxes with his funny ways. Over the years, there have been plenty of other characters who have brought something special to my life too.

Even if a cat becomes a member of my family through the cruelty of others, I'm thankful I've been given the opportunity to help that cat experience some love and comfort in his or her remaining days. There are many good people in this world, but the actions of the few cruel ones can have such a terrible effect. I don't like to dwell on that side of things, but there was one story that affected me and made me grateful for the cats I could truly help.

One day there was wailing at our back door, which I opened to find a bag of bones masquerading as a cat.

'Listen to this one,' I called to Chris. 'We'll have to call it Bob Marley, there's such a wailing coming from it!'

I didn't want to let the cat in straight away, as I didn't know how the others would take to her. We had an old barbecue that she sheltered in after a while, then she eventually made her way into the house. Bob Marley was clearly a very ill cat; there was something wrong with her that I couldn't put my finger on. Once she was as good as living with us, I took her to the vet. He told me she had kidney trouble but he also said that, as she was really someone else's cat, maybe they knew about this and she was getting treatment already.

I got a big blackboard and wrote a message on it to say that we had the cat; I described her, and asked if her owner recognized her, could they please get in touch? I put it at the entrance to the cul-de-sac where we lived. I felt it was the right thing to do, as someone could very well be distraught without this sick animal. I was willing to let her go if her owner contacted us.

A few days later, there was a knock on the door. I opened it to find a young boy, who, with no introductions, said: 'The cat's ours and my mum wants it now, so give it back.' I asked him if he knew that she was sick and needed medicine, but he just shrugged and repeated the message that I was to give her back – now. It was pouring with rain, but I put Bob Marley into one of my baskets and followed the boy back to his house. He shoved his front door open and left me standing outside, dripping wet, with the cat basket in my hand.

His mother came to see me, and snatched the basket out of my arms. 'Actually, that's my basket,' I said, although she clearly knew this. She stared at me, opened it, shook Bob Marley out and roughly handed the basket back to me. I repeated what I had said to her son about the poor cat being ill and gave her the medication we had bought. She didn't say a word.

On the walk home, the rain mingled with my tears and I felt that I'd done the wrong thing. Bob Marley wasn't our cat but what sort of life would she have with people who seemed to care little for her? I'd willingly take on the cost and trouble of looking after her. After a couple of hours, I'd cried myself out and managed to feel a little better.

Since this family had asked for Bob Marley back, they must have some feelings for her, I reasoned. I decided to go back and gently remind them about the kidney problems. When I got there, I could hear Bob Marley before I saw her. She was making her strange wailing sound and she had been kicked outside in the torrential rain. The little thing was soaked through. I huddled down to stroke her and I knew the woman was watching me from her window. Bob Marley wasn't my cat and there was nothing I could do about it. I said 'goodbye' and walked home, crying once more. I never saw Bob Marley again.

There is often heartache where cats are involved. You won't be surprised to hear that Clyde, who was so caring when Gemma was ill, had a sister called Bonnie. Bonnie's main hobby was to squeeze herself into the smallest space imaginable, in any sort of container, no matter how unlikely it seemed that she would get into it or how uncomfortable she appeared once she'd achieved her goal. As soon as she saw any basket or box, she would dash over and turn herself round and round and round, edging further and further in, until she'd managed to wedge herself into whatever confined space she'd found. She seemed to be able to get into things that were a quarter of her size, and she was very determined. She'd sit with her bottom stuck high up in the air with no space whatsoever.

Bonnie talked incessantly. She constantly yapped away, even while she was trying to get into her various small places. As she went round in circles, she'd yabber away to herself, as if she were either complaining about what a terrible bother these things were or reassuring herself that it could definitely be done despite the laws of physics. Even when she wasn't taking part in her favourite activity, she would chatter. If I was going about the house, cleaning or tidying, Bonnie would discuss matters with me and, if I didn't join in the conversation, she'd nip me quite hard, often on the hand, as if to say, 'I'm talking to you.' I laughed at her little reminders. I loved her character and the way she would spend hours trying to get back into the tiny place she'd left minutes earlier.

Cats have their own characters, just like people do, and you can build up a different, marvellous rapport with each one. Chris had his own relationships with the cats, and was particularly fond of Bonnie and Clyde, and Jack. Bonnie and Clyde always went looking for

Chris when he was away on the lorries: when he left, one of them would go out the front door to try to track him down, while the other went out the back. They were very close, which isn't always the case with siblings.

You always knew where Bonnie was with her 'yap yap yap' chatter, but one terrible morning after Chris had gone, I realized that I hadn't heard her for a while. I spent hours looking for her, going into every shop nearby, asking everyone, 'Have you seen my cat?' and describing the beautiful creature she was. The last shop I went to was a newsagent's, and, by chance, I bumped into the young lad who delivered the papers. I didn't have a photograph of Bonnie with me (I now keep a pile of photographs on my kitchen worktop, one of each cat I have, in case of such eventualities), but as I described her yet again, I saw his face drop.

'Oh no,' he said, 'I saw a cat just like that.'

'Where? What has happened to her?' I asked, scared of the answer.

The words were as bad as I'd expected. 'I'm so sorry,' he muttered. 'She was lying in the gutter in front of the hairdressing shop.'

That was the next one on my list. I ran along, but there was nothing (or no one) in the gutter. I went inside and asked the woman in charge if she'd seen anything earlier that day. She had; she'd called the council to come and collect the cat. I was convinced it was Bonnie.

It is one of the hardest things to deal with. When you lose a cat suddenly, your mind races through all the things you could have changed. *If only* I hadn't let her out that morning. *If only* Chris had been at home, she wouldn't have gone looking for him. *If only* she had gone in the other direction. Just one change, just one second later, and she would still be with me. I'd be at home, none the wiser, and Bonnie would trot in, yapping at me, trying to fit into the fruit bowl.

I ran out of the shop and rang the council as soon as I got home. I was eventually put through to the department I needed, and asked if a cat had been brought in. When I was told that one had, I asked, 'If she has a collar, could you please check her name?'

After a few minutes the man came back on the line and said, 'It says *Bonnie*. I'm sorry – is that your cat?'

Through the tears I told him that she was indeed mine, and asked what he would do with her now. He paused for a few seconds, then answered, 'The same thing we do with all of them, dear.'

'Which is?' I forced myself to ask.

'I'm sorry, dear, but we have to get rid of them.'

I wanted to scream.

This was a lost life; a creature had died too soon, too horribly. I felt panic kick in. 'No!' I shouted. 'Please, please don't do that. I can't drive but I'll get a taxi there as soon as I can. I need to say goodbye and I need to make sure she's treated properly.'

Thankfully, the man was extremely kind – perhaps my words had touched him in some way. 'Don't do that, dear,' he said. 'I'll bring her to you.' He took down my address and said he would come as soon as he could.

When he did bring her home to me, it took a while for me to pluck up courage to look at her but I hope what I found will be of comfort to others. It was quite amazing. There were no marks whatsoever on Bonnie, no indication that she was anything other than asleep.

I rang the vet to ask whether I could bring her in to be cremated and took her as soon as I could pull myself together. It was the last thing I could do for Bonnie; it's the last thing I can do for all my darling cats. I've never buried any of them in the garden but perhaps the reason I don't will seem silly. We move house so often that I'd feel I was deserting them – again. They would be left there alone, and the many souls we've shared our lives with would be without each other. I think it's better to know in advance what I will do when the sad day of farewell arrives. Each of them is treated in the same way and I can only hope that we will meet again one day. I try to help them, and I always love them, but sometimes my heart hurts from the loss.

CHAPTER 12

A Match Made in Heaven

When I married Chris, he'd lived in the same place all his life. He must have got quite a shock when he ended up with me, because I would move every month given half the chance. Perhaps it was because I'd been uprooted as such a young child, and never really felt settled, that I never felt the pull of one location or the sense that I never wanted to leave. I've loved all the homes we've set up together, but I'm not overly sentimental about them, because I know that a loving environment can be created anywhere and it has little to do with bricks and mortar. As long as I have my cats, I'm happy.

Although the children left long ago, and I'm now a grandmother, part of me still wants to create a perfect home – only now I'd be doing it for my kitties. So it was no surprise to anyone when I announced that I was looking for another place. Another move was on the cards – this time to Plymouth. I felt like a change of scenery, as I so often did. How could Chris and I have possibly known that this would be the place where one of our cats would become internationally recognized?

Casper was moving to a place that in many ways epitomizes English spirit and history. Plymouth is a beautiful city with a heritage stretching back more than a thousand years to Saxon times. The links between the land and the sea have played a large part in its history, with the city established on moorland to the north and the English Channel to the south. Rivers run through and across it, and its name comes from the River Plym to the east.

Farming land and communities at the mouth of the Plym can be traced to the Domesday Book of 1086. One farm mentioned there – Sudtone, which means South Farm – developed into Sutton Harbour, which became the centre of medieval Plymouth. For almost eight hundred years cargo has been leaving Plymouth, which became an important, busy and wealthy place as time went on. In 1254 its town status was recognized by Royal Charter, and in 1439 Plymouth was the first town in England to be granted a Charter by Parliament.

Trade blossomed, not only with other areas of England, but also across Europe. The times were not without their troubles, however. As frequent wars with France brought attacks on the town, barriers and fortifications were built; some of these can still be seen to this day. Plymouth's growth sprung from a combination of maritime development, trade and military importance.

Plymouth became enshrined in world history when Sir Francis Drake masterminded the defeat of the Spanish Armada and then the first ever circumnavigation of the globe from the town. Indeed, the familiar story of Drake casually playing bowls as the Armada sailed up the Channel in 1588 is said to have taken place on Plymouth Hoe. For many people, Plymouth is most celebrated for being the site from which the pilgrims who were persecuted for their religious beliefs in the early seventeenth century left for the New World on the *Mayflower* in the hope of finding freedom and tolerance, and established their own Plymouth community.

This remarkable history continued for centuries. I like to think that the spirit of adventure and love of travel that is so much a part of the city is what made Casper so loved. In him, the people of Plymouth recognized one of their own. He may not have been born there, he may not have lived there all his life, but he adopted the character of that fine old English city.

After much searching, we found a house we liked and moved to a place called St Budeaux, an area named after a bishop from Brittany (Saint Budoc) who founded a settlement here around 480AD. A small church was built, which was eventually dedicated to Saint Budoc. The village was taken over during the Norman Conquest. Like so much of Plymouth, St Budoc was mentioned in the Domesday Book – as a village known as Bucheside – and valued at the princely sum of thirty shillings, which was quite a lot of money in those days. Over the next few centuries, the name changed frequently before becoming St Budeaux. The area became well known in the sixteenth century when Sir Francis Drake married a local woman (Lady Drake was buried in the churchyard).

During the Civil War, St Budeaux and the surrounding villages swore their allegiance to the Parliamentarian cause and the church was attacked by the forces of Royalist Cornwall and used as a garrison. It was almost destroyed by the end of the war, and not fully rebuilt for many years.

As time went on, the parish grew in size. Growth increased with the construction of the Royal Albert Bridge and the development of roads throughout the nineteenth century. In 1899 St Budeaux combined with the town of Devonport, and by the start of the First World War it was amalgamated into the city of Plymouth. The Second World War resulted in many homes being bombed, and, once this period had ended, there was a huge rebuilding programme. There are many ex-forces houses in the area. St Budeaux is typical of many places in England – a mixture of housing, local shops, schools and community centres. It is very ordinary and very normal.

I think that is why so many people have been drawn to Casper. Had he been a grand cat from some posh country estate, or a pedigree cat who was groomed and pampered to within an inch of his life, would there have been so much interest? I don't think so. Casper was everyone's cat. He was an ordinary little moggy,

loved and beautiful, but the sort of boy who reminded
people of their own cats. I like to think that, as they read
or heard Casper's story, they looked at their own pets
and wondered what they got up to. Or perhaps they
wondered where Tiddles was when they were laughing about Casper's bus ride, then suddenly realized that
maybe Tiddles was up to the very same thing.

Casper was an extraordinary cat, while at the same
time he was a very ordinary one. His adventures made
people smile, and they were a novelty, but they were
also not so far-fetched that others couldn't imagine
their own cats getting up to similar naughtiness. This, I
believe, was Casper's charm. Everyone could love him,
and everyone could remember their own cats – past or
present – getting up to all sorts just like him.

As I settled into the new house in Poole Park Road,
all of this was ahead of me – and him. I had no way of
knowing that bringing Casper to Plymouth was going
to be a match made in heaven and that Plymouth would
take Casper to its heart. I unpacked boxes, kept an eye
on the cats, met new neighbours and had no idea what
was around the corner.

I managed to get a job working in a nursing home
with elderly people. I still couldn't drive but luckily
there was a bus stop directly opposite our new house.
I noticed that Casper was all too keen on crossing the
busy road, but there was only so much I could do about
it. If I had a day off, I would try to keep an eye on him
and make sure he was close to me, but on the days I

worked, he was left to his own devices. Given that I was never able to keep him in against his wishes, there wasn't much I could do to force him to stay indoors all day, but I did usually try to get him in before I left.

I've always kept up a running commentary with my cats and I would give Casper rules every day in the hope that he might finally pay attention to them. Now, Cassie,' I would chide, 'that's a very busy road out there and it's also very new to you. I don't want you going out there at all, but I know that you're going to ignore me, so I hope that at least you'll try to be safe. Look out for traffic, and only go across when it's all quiet.'

He always had a way of looking at me as if I were quite ridiculous – not to be talking to a cat, but to be considering that he might follow my instructions. He was a cat of leisure and a cat who wandered where he pleased. Why on earth would he be restricted because that was my preference? Still, I persevered with my words of warning in the hope that one day he would take pity on me and do as he was told.

One day in the summer of 2009, I was running a little late. Things had taken longer than usual that morning and everything had resulted in me being in rather a hurry. I gathered my things together and prepared to rush off to work. I knew that my bus was due, but I couldn't get Casper indoors. 'Casper! Casper!' I shouted outside, knowing full well that he was darting under bushes and shrubs every time I looked for him. 'Come here, now!' I was getting more and more desperate for him to come in, as I was worried that, should he see me leave, he would follow me.

It was no use. He wasn't going to come indoors and I was going to have to leave him outside for the day. The clock was ticking and I would miss my bus at this rate. Indeed, as I closed the front door behind me, I could see the bus I needed coming up the hill towards the stop – but I could also see Casper with his beady little eyes on me. It was a constant mystery to me how he could keep himself hidden until it was too late for me to take him back in, and he'd done it yet again. I was torn, but knew that I had to decide between going for him (and watching as he no doubt managed to evade me yet again), missing my bus and being late for work or heading off. I chose the latter. Casper watched me closely as I ran across the road.

I jumped onto the bus that had just arrived and breathlessly said to the driver, 'Can you go quickly, please?'

'Why, what's wrong?' he asked.

'I'm a bit worried about my cat,' I told him. 'He's a terrible one for crossing roads and I can see him watching me. It would be a nightmare if he came over here while I was getting on the bus.'

'Is that right?' he smiled.

'Yes,' I answered, 'so, please, do hurry.'

With those words, I sat in the seat behind the driver but on the other side. It was very close to him and I could see him clearly. He didn't seem in any rush to leave, despite what I'd told him, and he was still smiling. I couldn't quite believe what he said to me next, as I looked anxiously out of the window for Casper.

'The only thing you've got to worry about,' he laughed, 'is that you're sitting in his seat!'

He must be joking, I thought.

'What? You're having a laugh, aren't you?' I asked.

'No,' he replied, although he was still grinning. 'You live across the road there?' I nodded. 'You've got a fluffy black and white cat?' I nodded again. 'Well, I've got news for you – he likes buses, and he particularly likes that seat you're in, as that's where he naps pretty much every day when he goes on his jaunt!'

I had to get this straight.

'My cat – my Casper – comes on the bus? He jumps up onto a seat? He lies there, asleep, while you drive around? And I knew nothing about this?'

'No, not really . . .' he said, as I waited for the punchline. 'He isn't always asleep – sometimes he looks out the windows, sometimes he sits on a lap or two, sometimes he sits up the back.'

'And what do the other passengers say?' I asked.

'They accept it. Why wouldn't they? He's no bother – he's a lot easier than some of the people I get on this bus,' he chuckled. 'Never pays his fare though!'

I still thought he was having me on. I'd know if my cat was travelling on the bus – wouldn't I?

I spent the rest of the journey to work in a bit of a spin. I was torn between thinking this was just a joke but also

knowing that Casper did like vehicles, he did cross the
road a lot and he did disappear for hours on end. Could
this possibly be true? Was my cat really a day-tripper?

My head was full of what the driver had told me, and
I had no idea what to do. By the end of my shift, I had
a clearer idea, but how was I to know what I was about
to unleash?

CHAPTER 13

Casper the Travelling Cat

I went to work but spent the rest of the day in a real state. The bus driver had seemed genuine. If he'd been spinning me a tale, I don't think he would have kept it going. Surely, once he thought I'd fallen for it, he would have let me in on the joke and admitted he was messing about? He didn't seem to have any malice in him; he appeared simply to be passing on some information that I didn't know. I didn't mention it to anyone at work, and decided to wait until Chris called that evening to try to figure out what was going on.

When he rang from his stopoff point, my words sounded bizarre even to me. I told him what the driver had said and asked him what I should do. 'Well, do you believe him?' he questioned. 'Do you think Casper is getting on the bus, just as he says?'

That was the odd thing: the more I thought about it, the more I could see it was plausible. 'I think he might be doing exactly that,' I confessed. 'He's always crossing that road and I've seen him hanging about the shelter. He disappears for hours on end, and despite me trying to call him back or dangle turkey roll, he never appears. Then, all of a sudden, there he is. Chris, I think the driver might be telling the truth.'

Saying the words made it seem much more real. As I thought it all through and verbalized it to Chris, I could see, in my mind's eye, Casper getting on the bus, sitting there, napping and coming home when he felt like it. When I finished talking to Chris, I looked at Casper lying on the sofa, watching me with one eye open. 'Is that what you're really up to, Cassie?' I asked him. 'Are you leading a double life? I don't suppose I'll ever know,' I concluded.

I went to bed a little more settled but by morning had managed to think of a whole host of problems. Despite the fact that the driver I'd spoken to the day before had been so friendly, I was worried. He may not have had any problems with Casper, and the passengers he knew may have welcomed him, but there were concerns. If this was really happening, what if Casper was taken somewhere and got lost? What if he was frightened and couldn't find his way home, sleeping for ages until he was in a strange part of Plymouth? I now had more to worry about. I hoped I could get other people to help out.

I reasoned that if I contacted the main bus companies that used the route on Poole Park Road, I could ask them to watch out for Casper and perhaps even discourage him from boarding the bus in the first place. I didn't expect anyone to look after my cat for me, but I thought that by informing people I could alert both drivers and passengers to what was going on.

I sent a letter to one bus company in which I explained that I had just found out about Casper's adventures. I asked whether they could possibly warn their drivers about this travelling cat and ask whether they would try to discourage him from getting on the bus as I was terribly worried about him. I was polite and tried to let them know that I was only giving them some information that I thought might help them too – should any of them see a cat sitting on their bus without warning, they might be a little perturbed.

After some time, I received what I thought was a rather unfriendly reply in which I was told, 'If you permit the animal to stray from your garden, then you have to accept the consequences of allowing the animal that freedom.' Goodness! I had only asked that they be aware and perhaps show a little compassion, and for that I was being told off. The letter went on:

the drivers tell me that they are well aware of this cat's habits and that they are to some extent fed up with it. They have a difficult and responsible job to undertake at the best of times and having to remember to check their bus for a stray cat is not appreciated, especially when they are busy. I would respectfully suggest that you restrain your animal using a lead or tether to ensure that it is unable to stray

from your property . . . we will not be held responsible for
anything which may happen to it as a consequence of your
failure to control or restrain it.

I was then curtly informed that the photograph I had
sent them to help identify Casper was being returned
to me. I was a little shocked by the tone. The driver who
had told me what Casper had been up to had been so
nice and not seen it as a problem at all. I'd hoped that,
by warning other drivers, I'd be able to keep an eye on
Casper and warn them of an unusual cat they might
find asleep on a seat. I was upset that I was being told to
'tether' my cat in a fashion that would stop him walking around freely – surely if I did that I would be a very
cruel owner indeed? In fact, if I did that, I would have
expected someone to report me to the RSPCA.

By writing the letter, I hadn't been asking anyone to
take responsibility for Casper, I was simply asking them
to be vigilant. This was something I had done on other
occasions. For example, when our next-door neighbours
moved out and put their house up for sale, I'd popped
a note through the door warning the estate agent and
prospective buyers that they might find Casper in there,
so could they please make sure he wasn't locked in when
they left? I thought I was being a responsible owner, not
someone trying to shift the blame onto someone else if,
God forbid, something did happen to Cassie.

This letter had shaken me, but I then realized that the
company I had written to was not the one that employed

the driver who'd told me about Casper. I hesitated a while, wondering whether I would get the same reception if I called First Devon and Cornwall, but my need to do all I could for my cat was my primary concern, so I found the number for their office and called straight away.

The attitude there could not have been more different. The phone was answered by a chap who introduced himself as 'Rob from Customer Services'. As I spoke to him for the first time, I didn't know what a comfort and help he would become to me over the next few months. Rob would turn out to be one of the people in Casper's story who would always go beyond the call of duty – even if *he* thought he was just doing his job – and would prove to be immensely supportive.

I started to tell Rob what was going on and cautiously asked whether he could maybe warn the other drivers. 'I'm typing up a notice as we speak,' he informed me. 'As soon as I come off the phone to you, I'll print it off and put it up on the noticeboard and in the canteen.'

What a difference! Rob was as good as his word, and within minutes, the following notice was posted on the information boards:

TRAVELLING CAT

CAN ALL DRIVERS ON SERVICE 3 BE
AWARE THAT THEY MAY HAVE A FELINE
PASSENGER ON BOARD WHO HAS BOARDED

AT THE POOLE PARK ROAD AREA AND IS
TRAVELLING INTO TOWN. IF HE IS SEEN,
CAN THE DRIVER CALL CUSTOMER SERVICES
AND WE WILL CONTACT THE OWNER TO
MAKE HER AWARE HE IS SAFE AND WELL.
MANY THANKS – ROB

I've since spoken to Rob and he's told me that when I first called him, he thought it might be a prank, just as I had when I first heard about what Casper had been doing. He said that after two or three years in customer services, he's heard most things, but the idea of a cat popping on and off the bus seemed a bit far-fetched. 'I thought I'd go along with it,' he recalls. 'So I asked, "Where does he get on?" All of the things I asked Sue were answered with such openness that I started to think maybe this was true after all. There was so much personal information and she seemed like such a nice lady that I couldn't help but believe her and decided to do what I could to help out.'

To me, Rob is such a big part of this story because he, too, is one of those traditional British types who believes in manners and fair play and doing what you can to help people. As I've found out more about him, I've realized that he didn't treat me any differently to anyone else that day – he's like that with every person who calls his line. He always goes out of his way and he always does it with such a lovely manner that he reassures anyone he helps. He later told me that he was raised to believe that good manners cost nothing – a value he is passing on to his own children. He treats everyone as individuals. I was so lucky to have got him on the line that day.

Rob found that by the time his posters had been up for not much more than half an hour, the drivers were chatting about Casper, so he knew it was all true. The talk in the canteen that day was full of tales of the cat who rode the number three bus. Some of the drivers had mentioned it to each other in the past, when Casper started his antics, but it was as if Rob's poster had opened the floodgates and they all started discussing whether they had seen Casper on their bus, how often he'd been there, where he went, what seat he liked, what he got up to and all sorts of other things.

Over the next few days, I started to ask for a bit more information every time I took the bus and I gradually put together more pieces of the Casper jigsaw. The drivers didn't have much time to talk as there were always plenty of passengers getting on and off, but they always seemed to have a moment to tell me about Casper. I'd been promoted to the position of his mum rather than merely his owner and they were delighted to inform me of the misadventures of my boy.

It seemed as though every time I asked one of them whether they knew him, they did. No one was surprised when I asked the question, and it seemed that I was the odd one out for not knowing what was happening. How long had this been going on, I wondered? Many of them seemed to think it had been since we moved in rather than just a day or two before I discovered it. I was amazed. My cat had a secret life.

'That little chap's been on my bus for longer than I can remember,' said one, while most of them went for a vague 'ages' when I asked how long he had been travelling.

One woman told me that she always checked the internal mirrors before driving off from a stop, and the day she first saw Casper reflected in one of them she got quite a start. People leave handbags, newspapers and sweets on the seats, but she'd never seen a cat there before.

As I pieced everything together, I discovered that he liked to sit in the front seat where I had originally been or the back one where the noise of the engine was loudest. He was always perfectly happy to be stroked, tickled or even picked up by passengers. He was sometimes asleep before they moved off from the bus stop, and, most amusingly of all, he always waited in line. They all said that Casper was never at the front of the queue or the back. He waited between people, in the middle, and the other passengers seemed happy with that too, never pushing past him or jumping the queue. How British is that? We love our queues so much that we even apply the rules to cats. I was astounded.

Some of the drivers said that Casper would often wait in the bus stop but not always get on a bus when it came. It was as if he had his favourites or was waiting for one in particular. They joked that they got quite offended if he decided not to get on theirs, and they'd ask him, 'What's wrong with me, then?' One driver told me that he'd seen Cassie waiting in the shelter many times but he'd never once deigned to get on the bus he was driving – he wondered why he wasn't one of the chosen ones.

There was one part of the story that I found hard to get my head around. I had thought that Casper was probably staying on the bus for one stop, then jumping off and trotting back home again, but as they told me about his sleeping patterns, I wondered how long his trips were.

The number three went round Barne Barton before coming to St Budeaux. From the stop opposite my house, it travelled along the Wolseley Road to Camels Head, down Saltash Road past HMS *Drake*, St Levan Gate, Albert Gate, then on to Park Avenue through Devonport, where it would take the trip into the city centre. In the city centre, everyone would get off, the bus would travel up the end of town, turn round and then start the opposite journey all over again. It was quite a trip. 'Does he get off at St Budeaux Square?' I asked one driver. It was just over five minutes from where I lived.

'Are you joking?' he replied. 'Casper?' They all knew his name by now thanks to Rob's posters. 'That wouldn't be far enough for him, would it? Casper likes his little journey.'

'So, where does he go then?' I wondered, with my heart sinking. If he went any further than the Square, how would he know how to get home?

'He does the round trip,' I was told.

'He does *WHAT*?' I screeched.

'Oh yes, Casper likes to go into the city centre, then come back again – door-to-door service.'

'But the bus stops in the city centre, everyone gets off, the driver takes it to the end of the terminus and turns round to the other side of the road before letting anyone else on. Isn't that what happens?'

'Yes . . . usually,' came the reply. 'But Casper's different, isn't he?'

I was starting to realize that. 'In what way?' I asked.

'Well, we don't kick him off, do we? That wouldn't be right. Anyway, he's usually asleep – and we know where he wants to go. He's just coming back to Poole Park Road. We only ask the humans to get off. Casper gets special privileges – as I said, door-to-door service.'

I was speechless – again. Just what sort of creature was I sharing my life with?

CHAPTER 14

The Joys and Rules of Public Transport

Casper

❖

1 When leaving the house in the morning, ensure that your mum (or other human) doesn't see where you're going. Your travels are a personal matter. Humans are terribly inquisitive about what us cats get up to, and it's only right that we maintain an air of mystery about some of our activities.

2 You can comply with rule (1) by doing any of the following:

(i) sneak out when the human is doing their head fur, drawing on their faces, choosing what to wear, or one of the many other things they waste their time with each day; or

(ii) allow them to fuss over you for a while, make them think you are settled for the day and, when they wander off saying you're a 'good boy', saunter towards the door casually, then run like hell; or

(iii) ignore them totally as they attempt to keep you inside with threats, promises and compliments. This is the most effective - and satisfying -approach.

3 Cross the road to a bus shelter that has been previously selected for its proximity to home and availability of seating.

4 After careful perusal of the bus timetable (some secrets are just too precious to share, so please do not expect me to tell you how us felines access that sort of information), decide which vehicle you will grace with your presence that day. It is advised that you vary the times of buses and drivers you select, so as to make yourself slightly more mysterious and also to amuse yourself as the aforementioned drivers wonder why you never choose them.

5 Wait in line with the human passengers. This is very important. For some reason, said humans find it odd and amusing when cats share their transport. They are clearly the ones who are odd and amusing, for if they wished to retain such vehicles purely for their own use, why have open doors and comfortable seats? However, if you adhere to bizarre human rules relating to something called 'queues', they will change their minds and think your presence is completely natural. Humans are very keen on regulations, which is why they wash themselves only in the privacy of their own homes rather

than when they actually need to do so - and they admire any species who can do the same.

6 Do not draw attention to yourself by pushing to the front of the queue. Allow a human or two in front of you, and a few more behind. By taking up a position in the middle, barely anyone will notice you.

7 When you enter the vehicle, choose the seat that most appeals to you - from my research, I find a window seat to be most intriguing, as well as those towards the heating at the back of the bus. You may find that a human wishes to share the seat with you - this is unpleasant at times (see my previous comment on their washing habits - not all of them smell quite as fragrant as one would hope), but has to be accepted.

8 Should a human sit beside you, pretending to be asleep often works (I find that pretence is often not required as there is something about being on a bus that lends itself to a lovely little snooze). Some may be courageous enough to stroke or pat you - allow this. They are generally harmless, and I personally rather like them, so why not indulge their ways?

9 Ignore rules that are inconvenient or clearly not applicable to our species. I find that drivers on my chosen bus route shout at their fellow humans to get off once we reach what they call a 'terminus'. This does not suit

me. I wish to go back home at the end of my trip, not
potter around shops. I find that by ignoring such orders,
new rules - much better ones - can be put in place that
apply only to felines and allow us to get whatever we
want - which is the purpose of life, really.

10 When you have reached your destination (feel free to
stay on the bus for as long as you wish), alight at your
home stop, casually wander off, paying no heed to the
humans with gaping mouths who are scratching their
heads, and trot home to mum (or other human) for a
nice snack.

11 Cross your paws that no one gives the game away,
because if they do, oh dear me . . .

CHAPTER 15

Casper Conquers Plymouth

From what I learned, picked up from lots of little conversations, I don't think the drivers encouraged Casper to begin with, as they were concerned that he was going to get lost. He seemed to have just worn them down. As they always saw him in the same shelter, and they guessed that he lived nearby, they started to let their defences down. He was very fast and I don't believe he waited in the queue to begin with – his initial concern was to get on the bus quickly and be allowed to stay there. It was only once he had established his right to be on the bus that he remembered his manners. Once the drivers had seen him often, they let him get away with it. Casper had also been the subject of a lot of chat in the depot, and once the drivers knew they weren't the only ones letting him nap and giving him free trips, they didn't feel so bad about what they were doing.

As time went on, Casper's regular trips started to be noticed by passengers too. I later discovered that there were those who would pick him up when he got back to Poole Park Road if he showed no sign of waking up, and gently pop him into the shelter across from his house, before getting back on the bus and finishing their own journey. I was starting to get the feeling that there were a lot of good people around who were doing all they could to look after Casper when I wasn't there, and I was particularly grateful to the drivers.

One of the drivers said she often stopped opposite my house for her break, and she'd let Casper on while she waited or read her newspaper, but she was very nervous about driving off with him as she had no idea that he was doing this so often and he always found his way back home. Once her break time was up, she would collect Casper from whatever seat he had chosen and pop him back in the shelter, so he got a little time on the bus but she didn't have the worry of wondering whether he was going to get lost. It turned out that quite a few of the drivers were taking pictures of Casper on their mobile phones to show to family and friends who were a bit suspicious about whether this was actually happening.

I wanted to thank all the First bus drivers (the only buses Casper seemed to like) for what they had done and what they were continuing to do, so I decided to write them a thank you letter. Rob had originally put up posters in the depot, but I didn't know how successful they'd been nor did I realize that they were in a position where every driver would see them, so I hit upon the idea of using the letters page in my local newspaper to show my appreciation.

The *Plymouth Herald* is read by lots of people in the area. It's a daily publication and I'd seen many of the drivers with a copy beside them. Without thinking of the furore to come – how could I know? – I scribbled down a quick letter, briefly outlining what Casper was up to, and thanking everyone at First for their fantastic help. I suppose I also wanted other people to know how obliging the bus company had been, as readers were often quick to complain about things. It seemed like an efficient way to pass on my thanks as well as to recognize publicly all the wonderful people who were being so kind to me and Cassie. The letter read:

> *Thank you to First customer services and the*
> *drivers on the number 3 bus (Plymouth).*

I would like to personally thank Rob in customer services and all of the drivers who drive the number 3 bus route. Our cat, Casper, insists on boarding at Barne Barton and going for a ride. It appears he has ridden the complete circuit to the city and back home on many occasions, asleep on the seats.

He is a rescue cat so we have no idea where he originally came from but obviously he has no fear of buses! Thank you most sincerely to all the drivers for being so vigilant and kind to Casper. We appreciate it is a nuisance that our cat keeps getting on, so thank you for not putting him off in

any strange area. We don't want to lose him as he is old and
a very much-loved pet.

A few days later, I got a call from Rob to see whether I was willing for him to give my number to a local journalist who wanted to talk about Cassie. What was that all about, I asked him? He said that the thank you note I'd written to the letter page had been seen by someone and they thought the story was fantastic. Now they wanted to chat to me and see what else they could uncover. To be honest, I thought that was odd, but saw no harm in it. From finding it hard to believe that Casper had been getting on the bus at all, I'd now discovered from so many people that he was a regular – and happy – passenger that it almost seemed quite normal to me.

Only now do I know what was happening behind the scenes at the *Plymouth Herald*. At the newspaper, there is someone who is in charge of the letters page and who looks over everything to see if there are stories that should be followed up. Apparently, Casper's tale fell into this category and my letter was passed on to the news editor, who asked one of the journalists to set up an interview. This journalist had to go out to another story, so passed it on to a colleague called Edd Moore. Edd then called Rob for my phone number, which he gave out after checking with me. Rob also suggested that Edd get in touch with the PR department of First bus to see if they could help out.

The rest, as they say, is history. A whole network of people was falling into place, all of whom would be instrumental in getting Cassie's story out to the world. They would prove to be individuals with hearts of gold. If Edd hadn't followed the story up, if First bus hadn't been so helpful about telling everyone what was happening, if Rob had never written that first poster, the entire tale of Casper the commuting cat might never have come to light. That would have been terribly sad, as I know how much pleasure people have had in talking about him and what memories his presence conjured up.

Rob asked around in the depot to find out as much as he could about Casper's trips, and discovered that out of the hundred drivers (who swap routes quite frequently) most had come into contact with him. Rob told me that he was pretty impressed by Casper's antics, such as always seeming to know where to get off, but he'd heard some other funny animal tales in the past.

When Rob worked in Hertford, there had been a Jack Russell whose owner couldn't walk him because of illness, so the dog used to get on the bus every day for a little trip. Rob found out that there were times when Casper used to do more than one circuit, going back into town again even though the bus had returned to Poole Park Road. It wasn't that he was asleep, it was just that he fancied a longer trip out.

As long as Casper was happy, the drivers were perfectly content to let him stay there. There was, by now, a running commentary on Casper going on in the depot, and some drivers were a little jealous if he hadn't been on their bus or they hadn't been allocated the number 3 since we'd moved there.

It wasn't a surprise to me that Rob, like so many other people who became part of this story, was an animal lover. He had cats of his own, as well as rescue dogs, and couldn't remember a time in his life when there had been no pets. One of his most vivid emotional memories was of the time when, at the age of twenty-three and just married, his beloved Bearded Collie of fourteen years had to be put down. 'I was destroyed, absolutely heartbroken,' he recalls, 'and I think that anyone who has ever loved a pet knows exactly how they become part of your life, leaving a huge gap when they go. Winston had been there all through my teenage years and I'd told him all my problems. Your pets never judge, they just give comfort, and I don't think it matters what age you are when they go; the sense of loss is just overwhelming.'

It was this recognition of how close many of us are to our pets that I feel made Rob so open to Casper's tale. He'd previously sent notes around to the drivers to tell them that, should they hurt an animal by accident, they must leave a note, find the owner or take the animal to the vet. I hadn't realized until then that there is no law in this country to oblige someone who has a road accident with a cat to report it to anyone. If you run over a dog, you must tell the police or the owner, but cats are deemed somehow less important than dogs and there is no such obligation when they are involved. The official line on this anomaly is that the law considers that cats cannot be trained as dogs can, so their owners are not responsible for any injury or damage done by them. It was a point that would, sadly, come back to haunt me and one that I fully intend to do something about.

After I had agreed that Rob could pass on my number, I got two calls – the first was from a lady called Karen Baxter, who was in charge of publicity and public relations at First Group. Karen told me how much she loved what she had heard about Casper and was very keen to help out with any story. I was delighted by this. I had no idea what was going on or why anyone would be interested in my little cat, so I was more than happy for a professional to give me some advice. The next call was from Edd, the journalist, asking if he could come and meet Casper and me with a view to writing something in the *Plymouth Herald*. Again, I was willing for him to do so, but what, I wondered, could possibly interest all of Plymouth in my cat?

I didn't want any attention for myself. All I'd wanted was to say 'thank you' to people in a very low-profile way. I thought that Edd would probably come along and see that this was no story at all. How could he possibly make a headline out of it? I never dreamed it would go further. I only gave in to get some peace and quiet.

Chris was away during most of this. He knew that Casper was riding the buses, but he had no idea that the story was getting bigger. We laughed about a few things when he was home. We'd found out that Cassie only ever went on First buses, never the ones from the company that had been so rude to me when I asked for their help, and we joked that he had good taste. I did mention to him that Edd was coming, but, like me, he almost brushed it aside. Neither of us had ever had any dealings with the media, and we were rather naive about such things.

When Edd turned up, I was relieved that he was so friendly and straightforward. He fussed over Casper and chatted as we had a cup of tea. He told me that this was a lovely story that he was sure would appeal to the readers who were looking for a bit of light and happiness in the middle of quite depressing times. 'It gets people down when they just read miserable things day after day,' he said, 'and what Casper gets up to will really put a smile on their faces. We have to cover crime and burglaries and unemployment – it's just part of the job – but every so often it's lovely to have something to take the doom and gloom away.' Edd thought that Casper would manage to do just that.

The next day a photographer arrived to take a picture of Casper. I was horrified when they asked me to be in some photographs too – it was pouring with rain and I certainly didn't feel camera-ready. Casper was getting fidgety and he was very wet. He desperately wanted down, and I realized it was because there was a bus coming. As it came closer, I shrieked that it was the wrong bus. In my mind, it had to be a First bus that was in the picture, as those were the ones that Cassie liked; however, the photographer said it didn't matter, and started snapping away. Those pictures of Cassie with 'the wrong bus' went around the world, and are doing the rounds to this day – an inaccuracy that really bothers me.

The photographer finished up and left. Edd said that the story would be in the papers the next day but it turned out that something else happened, which meant it wasn't there when I looked. 'Never mind, Casper,' I said to him. 'It was never meant to be.' I knew that not all stories ended up in the paper, and I assumed that Casper's tale wasn't quite as important as other things. With all that was going on in the world, perhaps the editor had decided that the paper was better filled with rather more serious tales after all.

I didn't know whether to feel disappointed or not. I suppose I'd got rather carried away with the excitement of it all, even though I'd never felt that comfortable to begin with. Now that it had ended as a bit of a damp squib, Casper and I were back where we'd started – which was fine. We were happy then, we'd be happy now. At least I had information about what he got up to and many more new friends to talk to on the bus every day. I believed that the article had been passed over, and things would go on as before – how wrong I was.

CHAPTER 16

Five Minutes of Fame

When I opened the newspaper on Wednesday, 29 July 2009, I could hardly believe my eyes. Casper was in the *Plymouth Herald* after all, a few days later than we'd anticipated. Of course, I'd spoken with Edd; I'd known that he was going to write the story, but seeing it in black and white made everything real. There was my Cassie in the paper where all of Plymouth could read about his adventures. I later found out that because there had been an ongoing story about a different bus company that had taken over the headlines for a few days, they had thought it best to leave another bus story until there was more space. Now that time had come.

It felt surreal to see Cassie's story plastered over the pages of the *Plymouth Herald*. Edd's article read:

Do you think I'm handsome?

Where's my supper?

Can we watch *On the Buses* again?

Tuppence, Casper's best mate from the early days

Everyone loves a little Whisky at Christmas

The Nutty Girls: KP and Peanut

Jack wants to go travelling too

Chris and Gemma taking 40 winks

Clyde

At full stretch

Ginny

Gemma before her operation

Bird's Eye View

On alert

Patience is a virtue

Fame at last

Fares please!

Back of the No. 3

Can someone ring the bell please?

My favourite seat

Not sure about the view here

Our special day

My favourite driver, Rob

Rainy day in Plymouth

Carefree commuter Casper is a regular passenger

Meet Casper, the commuting cat who's fast becoming a celebrity on Plymouth buses. Regular users of First's number 3 service may recognize the fluffy feline, who has been driving his owner up the wall with his constant trips to the city centre.

The adventurous cat politely queues behind other passengers at the bus stop outside his Barne Barton home, then quietly trots on board and curls up on a seat for the ride. But far from causing mischief he has proved a hit with drivers and customers alike, who always make sure he returns home safely.

Casper's journey takes him from just outside his house in Poole Park Road to the final stop at Royal Parade and back, via St Budeaux Square, HMS Drake, Keyham, Devonport and Stonehouse.

His owner Susan Finden has only just found out about his antics – but First Group have been bussing Casper around for months.

Susan, who picked him out of a rescue home in 2002, said he had always been a free spirit; she named him Casper after the cartoon ghost when he immediately started giving her and husband Christopher the runaround with regular 'disappearing acts'.

The 65-year-old care worker said: 'He'd always go off and have a wander. Once I had to walk a mile and a half with a cat basket to bring him back from a car park.

'He does love people, and I don't know what the attraction is but he loves big vehicles like lorries and buses.

'We think he must have come from a travellers' site or a haulage yard because he's not scared of loud vehicles at all – or dogs.

'We think he's about 12 years old but he has no road sense whatsoever; he just runs out across the road to the bus stop.'

Susan found out about Casper's regular 11-mile round trips when he followed her to the bus stop one morning, avoiding passing vehicles by a whisker.

'The driver told me he gets on all the time,' she said. 'I couldn't believe it.

'He queues up in line with people and just sits patiently in the queue good as gold – it'll be "Person, person, person, cat, person, person."

'He seems to be picking First buses rather than the Citybus ones, but we don't know why.

'When the drivers do their turnaround they'll all check the bus and if he's on there they make sure he stays on for the return trip. Then local people will take him off when he gets to the right stop.

'I'm really appreciative to all the drivers for making sure he gets home safely; I'd hate to lose him.'

First's Karen Baxter said the firm had put a notice up in the drivers' rest room asking them to look after the rogue passenger if they spotted him sneaking on.

One female driver even has a photo of Casper on the desktop of her computer.

Ms Baxter said the company had no plans to charge him for his trips.

*'In cat years he's an OAP so he'd get a free bus pass
anyway,' she said, 'and I'm not sure we'd feel comfortable
selling a cat a Rover ticket.'*

*Driver Rob Stonehouse added: 'He usually just curls up
at the back of the bus. Sometimes he nips between people's
legs but he never causes any trouble.'*

Casper would not tell The Herald *the reason for his
trips.*

Edd's article had certainly done Casper justice, and I was
delighted to see that Karen from First had also spoken
to him. Everyone was being so friendly and supportive
in their comments. Casper had stayed in that morning
– perhaps he sensed that something was afoot – and
once I'd read the article myself, I read it again to him.
He seemed totally disinterested, but I was very proud
of him. 'You must be careful if you get the bus today,
Cassie,' I told him. 'You might be mobbed by autograph
hunters!'

I had a few friends call me up and we all joked about
my celebrity cat. They asked whether I'd be getting
him a minder when he made his trips to ensure that he
always got the seat he wanted and wasn't hassled by his
public. It felt lovely to have such warmth directed at my
cat, and later that day I thought that I would look at the
article on the Internet just to see his little face there too. I
logged onto the *Plymouth Herald*'s website and was absolutely amazed when, as I scrolled to the bottom of the
screen, I saw all the comments that people had left. Edd

later told me that most stories get about ten messages on the board from readers, but Casper had more than a dozen times that already.

Dee from Crawley said, 'I loved the Casper story. Thank you for putting a smile on my face and in my heart.'

Another local lady commented: 'This is so cute . . . I am allergic to cats and dogs but wouldn't mind Casper sitting near me even if I did spend the rest of the day sneezing!'

One person was quick to see that, while it may have been odd, it was still a story that showed the good hearts of so many: 'This article has put the biggest smile on my face! What a lovely story, and good on the bus company for keeping the little guy safe! He can happily have a seat next to me any day! Big smiles Plymouth, it's nice to see we still have a big furry heart!'

In addition to the sheer number of messages, I was amazed by how many were from outside Plymouth. I'd thought this story would be a local one, but the way that people can access news from anywhere in the world these days had put paid to that.

One lady, Marjanna from Toronto in Canada, said, 'I love this story, made my day! Go Casper, go!'

Sheila from Los Angeles joined in to comment, 'I love this story – a very cool cat. Animals are the best!'

Maybe these people were ex-pats who always checked the local paper and that explained why there were so many comments from abroad, or maybe we really were part of a global community now. It got stranger the further I read down the page. There were people commenting from all over the globe, as well as so many locals who said that they knew Casper, that he had frequently been on the bus with them and that sometimes he had even sat on their laps. One lady made a video that looked like Casper was singing 'The Wheels on the Bus' and put it on You Tube, where it received over ten thousand hits.

This little cat of mine had a whole other life. Now that he was quickly becoming a celebrity, I hoped that I would find out even more about his adventures. If people knew that they hadn't imagined seeing a cat on the bus beside them as they went to work or into town, perhaps they would let me know how far he went, what he got up to or anything else that would help me complete the jigsaw.

Some people – although very few – made negative comments, usually about the health and hygiene issues of allowing a cat on public transport. That made me cross. Were they perfect? Did they think that all the people who got on a bus were shining examples of cleanliness? However, before I could get too annoyed, I noticed that others were making these arguments for me, and plenty of readers were sticking up for Casper's right to travel.

Life is short, stop moaning and groaning. All God's crea-
tures are precious and this is a lovely story about a cat who

just wants some excitement, attention and a dry day out of
the rain. Thanks, Casper, for putting a smile on millions of
readers' faces if only for a second before they turn the page
and read what the moanies and groanies thrive on.

JJ of Devon

Another local commented: 'I can't believe you people moaning about a cat catching a bus. Is that all your sad lives revolve around? I can't believe people are moaning about having to pay 50p for their dog – come on, are you that tight? Keep it up, Casper, enjoy yourself!'

The friendly comments were lovely, but there was also something really heart-warming about these complete strangers taking Casper's side. People were saying how happy they felt to read a story like this, because it was a welcome break from what usually hits the headlines. When I spoke to Edd at a later date, he said that this was what he had felt from the outset too. It had been a normal day at work for him, and he needed something to balance the crime and horrible recession tales, so the notion of a cat who rode the bus seemed quirky. How was he to know what would happen next?

As Casper's travels were being read about all over Plymouth and online across the globe, he was also grabbing the attention of Fleet Street. National newspapers were picking up on the story, and it had even been noticed by the Press Association, who sell articles to pretty much every media outlet. I, of course, knew nothing about this side of things – yet. The day passed in a bit of a blur. I spent the day answering calls and emails from friends and family about Casper, and I read the story to him again. He showed very little interest the second time round too; I suppose he already knew it all first-hand. I gave him an extra cuddle that night for being such a good boy while all of this was going on around him. When I settled him in for the evening, I whispered, 'There you go, Cassie, that's all the excitement over. You can just go back to your normal little trips now you've had your five minutes of fame.'

Who would have known how naive my words were? You'd think I'd have learned by now, but as I went to bed that evening, I had no idea what we were both in for the next day.

CHAPTER 17

Casper Goes Global

'Our Casper story goes worldwide!' screamed the *Plymouth Herald* the next day – and it was true. The story had exploded.

Casper the commuting cat became a worldwide celebrity within hours of appearing in The Herald. *We yesterday reported how the carefree feline regularly travels around town on First's number 3 bus from his Barne Barton home. Having proved a hit with drivers and passengers, Casper's story has captured the attention of media far and wide. The headlines came thick and fast as the Plymouth puss featured on websites from England's tabloids to the USA's mystate-line.com. The* Sun *declared that 'Stowaway Cat gets bus-ted', while The Press Association went with 'Joyrider Casper given a puss pass'. Teletext merely stated: 'Cat enjoys free bus rides'. He also appeared on a diverse range of other websites including Yahoo, Virgin Media,* The Sheffield Telegraph, Bury Free Press *and thisislancashire.*

I did a quick search and found the story on the BBC website, the *Daily Telegraph*, and the *Daily Mail* – they had all picked up on what Edd had written and put their own twist on it. Some papers had even covered the tale in their editorial columns, usually with excruciating puns. They were all very positive and kindly disposed towards Casper's hobby, and I felt as if he were being taken to the hearts of the nation. People from the four corners of the world commented on online versions of the story. The story was taking on huge proportions.

The response that day was incredible, but it was nothing compared to a few days later, when he appeared in newspapers and websites in Holland, Australia, India, China and South Africa. A newspaper in New York said:

Not all pets prefer to travel by foot – some find taking public transportation a better way to get around. In the English city of Plymouth, 12-year-old Casper the cat has been surprising his fellow commuters by riding the bus by himself.

No one was more surprised by all of this than me.

By the end of the day after Edd had published his first article, I felt like I was living in the middle of a whirlwind. I almost expected a public relations guru to call, offering to represent Britain's newest star. My address was very easy to find because of the mention in the paper, and my telephone number quite simple to get too. As a result, the phone never stopped ringing.

I found myself agreeing to all sorts of people coming to meet Casper for more interviews and filming. I was doing what I had done all along, which was to agree to things for an easy life. I'd had such a positive experience with Edd that I became less wary of dealing with journalists. Thankfully, I never had this positivity challenged, and everyone who has dealt with Casper's story from beginning to end has been a delight.

I wasn't keeping track of what I was agreeing to and a few days after the *Plymouth Herald* piece, I woke up one morning with butterflies in my tummy. It didn't take long to realize why: I'd said that I would give some interviews to *Today* and even do some filming with Casper for news programmes, and everyone was scheduled to come at pretty much the same time. So much for my organizational skills!

I pulled on some clothes and managed to get downstairs just as the doorbell rang. Standing outside was a whole gang of people, all jostling for my attention, all calling my name and asking for Casper. There was a film crew from the BBC and the director of First Devon and Cornwall. As well as Karen, the PR lady, and Jo, her assistant, there was a filming team from another BBC section called 'Spotlight', Devon Radio, photographers, journalists and goodness knows who else. It was pandemonium as they debated who would film what and when.

Thankfully, Karen from First bus had arranged for one of their drivers to come along to stand in some more pictures, as I hated that side of things. This young chap was also called Rob, and he got on very well with Casper. As they stood there, posing for the photographer, I did have a slight fluttering in my tummy about how many people seemed to be interested already, but I told myself that whatever was going to happen would happen, and there was nothing I could do about it. It still didn't seem that important, which was partly due to the friendliness of everyone; they made it seem so natural that it made me think that everything would calm down very soon.

A young chap, who turned out to be from the 'Spotlight' team, stepped forward and introduced himself. He said that a bus had been arranged through Karen, and they were hoping to take Casper on it for some filming. I was a bit shell-shocked but agreed. They were like bees round a honey pot. Then I suddenly realized that I had no idea where Cassie was.

I looked round frantically and was relieved to see one of the photographers lying on the floor with him, tickling him and being ever so friendly. He had such a way with Casper that I felt fine about turning my attention to the others while I heard the young man's camera clicking away. As I kept talking, he quietly picked Casper up and smiled at me, whispering that he was going to get on a bus with him. I felt quite relieved that my celebrity cat was being taken away from all the madness so I wouldn't have to worry about him getting spooked while all these people were here.

By the time he brought Casper back, I'd done lots of interviews and was starting to feel guilty that I didn't have something new to tell each person. The honest truth was that I didn't really know what Casper got up to every day; in fact, since the story had run, I was finding out more than ever before. Everyone said that I was doing well, but by the time I had to pick Cassie up and get on the bus with him for some filming, I was shattered. I'm no film star and I'd never thought I'd be signing up to have my face on screen first thing in the morning.

Driving round the number three route was odd. There were no real passengers; instead the bus was full of journalists and photographers all desperate for their piece of my little cat. We did a few circuits so that they could all get the shots they wanted. By the end, I was happy to collapse at home, with Casper in my arms. As I put the kettle on, I laughed at the fact that he looked exhausted too, and certainly showed no inclination to go on another of his daily bus rides.

'Well, Cassie,' I said to him, once I had a cup of tea and he had some turkey roll, 'that was certainly a very odd morning, wasn't it? I'm not sure you and I are cut out for this lark. Never mind, it's back to real life for us now. You've had your five minutes of fame.'

If I believed things would stop there, I was proven totally wrong. Once the new newspaper articles were published and the news clips aired, I started to get letters from all over the world. People were so drawn to Casper and his story, they wanted more information, more snippets from his life. It was also as if he were filling some terribly sad void that many of them had in their lives, as they told me of pets they had lost, families who had moved on, loneliness that filled their days.

One lady wrote:

Since I read about Casper, I cannot help thinking about the cats I have had over the years. We had kittens in the family when I was a little girl, and I've always liked having a cat to come home to. I lost my husband of fifty-six years last Christmas, and our lovely tabby Hetty had died a few months earlier. Now that all of my children are grown up with families of their own, I would love another cat to keep me company but I just cannot have one. I don't have long myself, and I would feel it so unfair to leave behind a cat or to think that one of my children felt forced to take it in. The story of Casper brought a smile to my face – as well as a few tears, and I wish you many happy years with him.

These were lovely sentiments. I was delighted that people were taking time out of their busy lives to write to me; the least I could do was repay the compliment. I wrote back to every single person who contacted me by post, and tried to tell him or her interesting little things about Casper, so that they would feel as if they knew him.

The media coverage continued: I was contacted by women's magazines, pet magazines, columnists and websites. Casper's fame was growing, but he was the same cat to me. He was still naughtily stealing food, not always washing, not paying attention to me and disappearing for hours on end. At least I now knew what he was up to when he disappeared. One of the newspaper articles worked out that if the drivers were telling the truth about how often he was on the bus and how far he rode, he had already travelled about 20,000 miles.

The stories kept coming and I was getting to hear more and more, although the information came in snippets. People all over Plymouth were talking about Casper. One woman I knew who worked on the taxi buses, was laughingly discussing his adventures when a passenger said that she saw him lots and had never really thought anything about it until she read his story in the paper. That appeared to be of the experience of many locals. Perhaps it's part of the British desire not to get involved. If Casper's appearances on the bus were treated as normal by everyone else, then no one wanted to be the first to draw attention to him. So, in turn, everyone thought it was fine, and Casper believed that he was entitled to go about his daily journey without interruption. I was so lucky that he always seemed to be meeting the right people and that he had never once come across some 'Jobsworth' who thought that little Casper shouldn't be on public transport and kicked him off.

The Casper phenomenon was particularly strange for Chris, as he wasn't around very often. He had to take long-distance jobs as and when they came up; he never knew if he would be in Scotland or Spain from one week to the next. He would tell people a few bits and pieces about what our strange cat was up to, but, to begin with, they all thought he was pulling their leg. Once they started reading about it in the *Sun*, the *Guardian*, and pretty much every other paper in the country, they realized that, bizarre though it may have sounded, he was telling the truth.

Once, when Chris was driving to France, he had the radio on and heard Sarah Kennedy on Radio 2 talking about Casper. That's my cat, he thought proudly. It didn't change their relationship. Cassie didn't suddenly develop airs and graces; he was still the same boy who jumped into the car beside Chris as soon as he pulled into the drive after a trip away.

Casper made people happy: me, Chris, the drivers, everyone who read about him. Despite the redundancies, the constant talk of recession and the unemployment figures rising, he put a smile on people's faces. Rob said to me at one point that life's just too serious. Lightness helps us all and you need to find happiness wherever you can. Casper gave everyone a bit of a break and reminded us that we can still find a bit of fun in our day-to-day lives.

He was taking it all in his stride but I wished that someone had told *me* what to expect and how to deal with it. There seem to be no guidelines handed out to people who are suddenly thrust into the media spotlight, and I would have welcomed some dearly.

CHAPTER 18

How to Deal with Fame

Casper

1 Assume that everyone is a good person - yes, they may want to write a story about you; yes, they may want to take your photograph, but as this will not interfere with the important things in life (such as riding buses or napping), allow them access. After all, it's no skin off your whiskers.

2 Do not be embarrassed or shy about the barter side of the deal - every celebrity has their price and, in my experience, most journalists are perfectly happy to engage in a spot of belly-rubbing, ear-scratching or coat-brushing to prove that they are fundamentally decent, if misrepresented, individuals.

3 Leave all the tricky stuff to your person - in fact, don't even concern yourself with the things that take up so much of their time, such as deadlines, phone calls and suchlike. A cat may have nine lives, but none of them is meant to be stressful.

4 Give your person a little comfort in return - they seem
to become inordinately stressed about the way in which
their head fur should be fashioned, whether they are
required to paint bright colours on parts of their faces
and if their costume is 'just right'. When they seem
to be running around not achieving anything, jump on
any pile of clothes they have discarded and roll on your
back. They will be delighted, even if such delight seems
to result in them running about even more and shriek-
ing a little.

5 When the doorbell rings, run away - you may even wish
to 'hide' somewhere they can see you quite easily, but
find themselves unable to access. I'm sure that everyone finds this as funny as I do.

6 If you are expected to perform - for example, I have been
asked to pose for pictures beside the wrong bus, and
board a bus when it is clearly not the one I'm waiting
for - be gracious. You will be repaid very soon, usually
in the form of turkey roll and cuddles.

7 After a while, when the attention has quietened down,
your person will invite you to 'listen to this', or 'come
and watch this'. For these purposes, you are expected to
sit beside them while they read to you from a newspaper
or put the noisy picture box on. Every so often, they
will say your name excitedly, showing the simple side
to their nature, for we know that the more interesting

activities would be to roll on the newspaper or hit the picture box with our paws every time something moves.

8 Do not change your behaviour - this is not because people will say that fame has gone to your head, but because dogs will laugh at you. Need I say more?

CHAPTER 19

Joining the World of Celebrity Cats

Of course, Casper wasn't the only cat who had gained fame for his travels, nor was he the only one who had discovered the pleasures of riding on the bus. A couple of years before Casper became famous, I read about a white cat called Macavity, who was in the papers because he liked to get on the bus from Walsall to Wolverhampton most mornings and ride for 400 metres to his favourite fish and chip shop. Passengers commented that he was the perfect passenger: he was quiet, minded his own business and never distracted the driver – just like Casper. I wondered whether he and Macavity had known each other at some point earlier in their lives and discussed their love of buses.

They weren't the only cats who had hit the headlines. I recalled reading about another called Kofi who'd gone missing for nearly four years. His owner had moved house from Nottingham to Sheffield, and, though she desperately missed her lovely cat, she'd given up hope of ever seeing him again. Little did she know that Kofi was both adventurous and determined. After he was picked up by the RSPCA wandering around Ipswich, looking lost and undernourished with an infected flea bite, they checked to see if he was microchipped. He was, and was soon reunited with his delighted owner. I guess that Casper clocked up a lot more than the 120 miles Kofi was estimated to have gone in his travels, but he did much of it in the luxury of a number three bus.

Plenty of other cats have been returned to their human families years after going missing, such as Dixie from Birmingham who took nine years to find her way back. Her mum said that her personality hadn't changed one little bit since the day she disappeared, but I wonder whether these creatures have experiences that scar them in one way or another. For a domestic cat to survive in the wild for such a long time is a miracle – perhaps they are taken in at some point by another family, or perhaps they are the lucky ones. Whatever happens, it always lifts my heart when I read or hear of another little moggy finding its way home to the ones who love him or her.

Perhaps the most impressive journey of all that I've heard of was that of Sandi, the ginger and white cat from Portsmouth. When he went missing one Friday, his owners were frantic because he'd never disappeared before. They handed out leaflets and put up posters everywhere, hoping against hope that someone would have information about where he was. They couldn't quite believe it when they got a call three days later to say that Sandi had indeed been found – in Spain!

He had been discovered onboard a P&O ferry, *The Pride of Bilbao*, on a Saturday night sailing from Portsmouth to the Spanish port. It was thought that Sandi got into a car that had then driven onto the ferry, then hopped out when it arrived in port. Thankfully, he had been chipped and was returned to his owners, otherwise the poor thing would probably have been put down, as no one would have known where he'd come from or whom he belonged to, and there may have been a fear of rabies. As it was, he was treated like a VIP, with a cabin to himself for the return journey home and meals of chicken and salmon. One report said that most of the staff had been in to give him a cuddle and would be sad to see him go.

Although there are always bad apples in the bunch, Britain is generally a nation of animal lovers, and I find that we do reach out our hearts to cats, dogs and all sorts of other creatures. When we stumble across them by accident, and somewhere we don't expect to see them – a bus or a chemist's shop, for example – it's such a lovely surprise that I believe our good nature takes over and we can't help but show kindness and affection.

Once Casper's story started to get so much attention, I became interested in finding out more about other creatures who'd undertaken strange trips. I found more than I could have imagined and I'd love to share a few of them with you.

Throughout history, cats have done the most amazing things. Often their journeys are undertaken not out of curiosity or because they are lost, but to meet more basic needs, such as finding their kittens.

Over a hundred years ago, there was one remarkable creature called Daisy. Although apparently born in Ireland, Daisy was left at a transportation company in Oswego, New York, by some passengers who had left their homeland in 1871. Daisy was regarded as a welcome addition to the buildings, as she was an excellent rat catcher.

Rather like a lot of ladies with careers, Daisy was caught out by nature. One day it was discovered that she had given birth to two kittens, but, for some reason, she had disappeared. This was very strange behaviour, as the babies were barely a week old.

Daisy had been known for her lovely nature and diligence, so it seemed very peculiar that she would go against what her body would be telling her and abandon her little ones. One gentleman who worked for the transportation company, the rather appropriately (or inappropriately) named Mr Pigeon, took the kittens home and tried to raise them. Sadly, without their mother's attention or milk, they died.

Many, many weeks later, one of other workers in the company was crossing a bridge at the depot when he met – as is reported in a journal of the time – 'the living skeleton' of Daisy. The same report tells that she was covered in mud, torn and bruised, with her tail almost worn off. She headed straight for the office where she had left her babies all those weeks ago and 'wauled' for them. Her poor heart must have broken as she searched high and low for the little mites who had by then passed on. She was comforted by those who worked at the company but she wouldn't settle.

Some time passed, and a ship came in from Ogdensburg, a place one hundred miles north-east of the depot. The captain saw all the fuss that was being made of Daisy and informed the workers that when he'd last left Oswego, he'd found Daisy was on his ship by mistake. He had put her ashore in Ogdensburg, not knowing what else to do. Apparently, she'd walked all the way back to Oswego, where she'd left her babies, no doubt panicking the whole way over the fate of her little ones. It may have happened well over a hundred years ago, but the power of a mother's love comes across to this day. I so wish that Daisy's tale had a happier ending.

More recently, a little male cat called Kuzya, who lived in Siberia, had the most amazing journey. He was only two years old when his family lost him. They were living in another part of Russia for the summer holidays and thought the best thing to do was to take Kuzya along, but he ran away in a place called Yakutsk before they returned home to Olenyok. Incredibly, he turned up on their doorstep three months later – thin, exhausted, with bite marks and his claws worn away to almost nothing. Kuzya's trek home had involved him walking 1,300 miles across Siberia, through woods and hills, crossing rivers and lakes – which rather puts Casper to shame!

Kuzya was by no means the widest travelling moggy, although he did seem to do it all by paw, unlike a kitty called Clyde from Tasmania in Australia. Clyde had been given to a little girl for her birthday, but had wandered off one day. The family got another cat, which unfortunately was run over. They decided they were unlucky and pets weren't for them – until three years later, when they received a call from a vet in mainland Australia 2,500 miles away. Clyde had been found by a local nurse five months earlier when he'd wandered into a local hospital. She'd taken him home, but when she was moving house, she went to the vet to see if he could be re-homed. The vet discovered he had been chipped and could be returned to his original family. It seems likely that Clyde must have done some of his travelling by car or van, as it was such a long trip – and he made the return trip home by plane.

The capacity of cats to survive is unbelievable. One that was locked in a Cadillac by accident ended up being shipped from the US to Australia. The cat managed to survive for fifty-two days without any food, simply by licking engine grease and eventually eating the car's instruction manual. I suppose that those were the only options available to the poor little thing.

Other cats have also had no choice but the most awful of options. A few years ago, a woman in California started to feed a group of feral cats near where she worked.

They got to know her, and often ran to see what treats she had for them. Over time she started to distinguish one from the other and identify the various characters. She became concerned about one when she realized his whiskers had disappeared – they looked as if they had been burned off. When she investigated further, she noted that there was a big chunk missing from the fur on his rear leg, almost as if it had been bitten off.

The next morning, this young black and white male was in an even worse state. His entire left paw was missing. The lady contacted a pet rescue service and, together, they worked out what was happening. This little soul was gnawing off parts of his body that had been injured. He was slowly dying, even though he was trying to save himself the only way he knew how. It was vital that he was captured and helped.

Every day he came to breakfast and managed to evade capture with the help of his mother, who would stand guard as he ate breakfast. The infection would surely kill him. He had chewed at his feet so much that the front left leg was gnawed off almost to the shoulder, and the right rear leg to the knee. The fact that he was still eating and still trying to save himself was testament to an incredible survival instinct.

Finally, by following the cat, who was by now being called 'Stubbs', and his mum to where they slept, and with the judicious use of some Kentucky fried chicken as bait, they managed to capture him, take him to hospital and treat the injuries. It transpired that someone had set fire to him in a hideous act of cruelty. All four of his feet and lower back legs were terribly burned – so much so that the pain of gnawing them off had been more bearable than leaving them alone. Eventually, even with help, he did lose a back leg up to the knee, a front one to the elbow and a toe from the front, but his amazing will to live, a great deal of medical care and a new home meant that there was a happy ending.

These extraordinary stories show how determined and brave cats are. Casper was only one of many, and I'm sure there are hundreds of others with similar tales. What I was quickly discovering was that his adventures were making people open up about the many wonderful creatures who had shared their lives too.

One lady from Edinburgh wrote to me to say that, some years ago, she had got two little kittens from a rescue centre. She named them Harry and Maisie, and became very fond of them as they grew. The two were completely different characters, despite being siblings. While Harry liked nothing better than to sit by the fire or on this lady's lap, Maisie was never one to enjoy cuddles and seemed to come home only for food, sometimes disappearing for days on end.

The woman and her husband were planning to move house, and about a week before they left, she decided to prevent Maisie from going out. The cat was going walkabout for such long periods that it was possible she wouldn't be back in time for the move if she got out. After three or four days, there was a knock at the door.

Standing there was a burly man, who asked whether Maisie was at home. The lady had closed the door behind her to stop the cat from escaping and was rather bewildered by this request.

'How do you know my cat?' she said.

'Everyone knows your cat,' he replied.

It transpired that the man worked in a haulage business nearby and went on trips across Britain (Chris laughed when I told him this story). Maisie had been going with him on many of these journeys since she was a little kitten. Although she had popped into the cabs of other drivers, this man was her favourite. He'd become worried when she hadn't turned up for a few days. He'd been on a trip to Nottingham and had fully expected Maisie to accompany him.

When the lady told the man they were moving, he seemed terribly upset. Maisie had been his little companion for so long and he would miss her. She wondered whether she could bear to leave Maisie behind, but she loved her too, and Harry would feel strange without his sister.

Once they moved to a rural area of Scotland, Maisie never wandered again. She settled into her new environment and became a hunter rather than a traveller. I teased Chris and said that I hoped he wasn't being unfaithful to our cats by taking others on trips when he was working.

Cats are such individuals and they are so good at finding their way into our hearts that I don't think I'll ever be surprised by any feline adventure story I hear. They are courageous and wise, brave and sometimes foolish, warm and caring, but always, always their own masters. There was a part of me that hoped Casper's notoriety would keep him safe so I could breathe a little easier than I had in the past.

CHAPTER 20

Nine Lives and Counting . . .

The road had always been my greatest fear. Although Tuppence and Peanut were very good and tended to stick to the gardens when they did go out, Casper was different. Despite speed bumps being put in place, they didn't seem to make any difference on Poole Park Road and cars drove along at a terrible rate. There were buses every ten minutes or so, and those were obviously Casper's main interest. Every time I heard an engine, I'd worry.

After Casper's story hit the headlines, my worry was tempered a little. Now that so many people knew about him and his antics, they were watching out for him. I fervently hoped that this would prompt them to drive carefully along the road just in case 'that cat' was on his travels.

After his brush with fame, I started to watch Casper more closely to try to build up a picture of what he got up to, but apart from his bus travels, he didn't go that far. When he wasn't in the bus shelter or on the bus, he spent most of his time in the garden watching the world go by. However, his obsession with vehicles was showing no sign of abating and I worried that he would go off in a van or a car given half the chance.

One morning in mid-November, one of the smaller buses on our local route broke down opposite the house. This wasn't one of the First vehicles that Casper loved so much, but I was worried that he would take too much of an interest in it. Immediately, I sensed there could be trouble. Casper was so nosy that he got up from his watching spot straight away and went over to the shelter. I kept an eye on him for a while, just to make sure he was still there. He was sitting perfectly still with the driver, who must have been waiting for assistance.

After a little while, two breakdown trucks came and I thought to myself, *here comes trouble.* I kept trying to coax him back with his favourite turkey roll, but it had no appeal compared to the motor show he was watching from the bus shelter. Eventually, after I'd been swinging slices of the stuff around for ages, he ambled across as if he was doing me an enormous favour. I closed the door quickly behind him and determined to keep him in until everyone had left.

Somehow – and I was never quite sure how Casper achieved this so frequently – he managed to escape. He must have got out the back, as the front exit and windows were completely sealed, but there was nothing I could do because, by the time I noticed he'd gone, the broken-down bus had been towed away, the breakdown trucks were gone and Casper wasn't waiting at the bus stop.

I started to panic as the day wore on and there was no sign of him trotting home. 'Where are you, Casper?' I kept asking, even though there was no one to hear me. I started to worry that he had gone off in one of the vehicles. Remembering that the broken-down bus had belonged to a company called Target, I got the number of their head office in Cornwall and asked for help.

'Please,' I begged, 'please can you keep a lookout for my cat?' I told them what he was like, how much he loved cars, lorries, buses, anything, and described to them the scene earlier when he had been so intent on watching the breakdown people. I asked if they could ask anyone who might have been there that day, and they suggested that I email a photo so that if he did turn up in the yard they would know it was Casper.

The afternoon turned into evening and still there was no sign of him. I started to wonder if he had got on a First bus and become confused, so I rang Rob in customer services, as he had always been so helpful. I was frantic by the time I asked him to please put out another notice asking the drivers to be alert for Cassie. He couldn't have been more obliging and typed up the poster as we talked.

Nothing happened and I spent the whole evening running between the front and back doors, calling his name, desperate to hear his little collar tinkle. By midnight, I was exhausted and knew that I had to go to bed. I suspected that he was well and truly lost, but there was nothing I could do in the dark and I would need my strength come daylight, when I would search for him until I could walk no more.

I opened the front door one last time and there he was. I cuddled him, scolded him, kissed him – every emotion was swirling around in relief that he was finally home. He seemed exhausted and I noticed that his pads were burning hot. 'Oh Casper,' I cried, 'what's happened to you, my darling?'

I'd always been so worried that something awful would occur and now it looked as if it had. When I took him into the light, I could see that his pads were bright red and all I could think was that he had indeed got on the broken-down bus or one of the breakdown trucks and then was spooked. Perhaps he realized that he was on an unfamiliar route or got a fright at some point, but I think he must have got off somewhere he didn't recognize and then spent the day walking home.

Usually when he came back, he went straight for something to eat, but this time he flaked out on the floor as if he couldn't move a muscle. He was flat out as I brought some food to him. He struggled to lift his head so that he could eat lying down, but he was so weak that he could barely do even that.

It was a terribly close incident; it was only his amazing homing instinct that had brought Casper back to me. He remained tired for a while, and though his pads recovered, he seemed reluctant to go out for a few days.

His tendency to go walkabout remained undiminished, however. On another occasion, one of the First drivers asked me when I was going to work whether Casper had got home all right the day before. I said he had, but what had made him ask? 'Well,' he said, 'he got on as usual but someone must have scared him or thrown him off the seat, because he got off at a stop that wasn't one of his usual ones.'

He got home in one piece then but I was starting to feel as if every time Casper went out that might be the last time I'd see him. There was a constant fear that he would jump in a delivery van and the driver would unwittingly take him away without even knowing he was there.

I tried so hard to discourage him from crossing the road, but how can you stop an animal who has his independence? I don't know what his life was like before we got him, but perhaps he was always on roads. Cats are so free spirited; our fears may just be the price we have to pay for their companionship. I'd have to lock Casper in and tie him up to stop him from going out – and, believe me, I've been tempted.

Casper broke the cat flap twice; he completely smashed it while I was at work. I got home to find a scene of mayhem and a missing cat, which proved to me how determined he was when he put his mind to things. It was as if he couldn't bear to be a prisoner. Given that he was so light-footed, there were times when he managed to sneak past me without me having the slightest notion that he had done so. I'd be sitting quite happily on the sofa, thinking how well

I'd done to keep Casper in that day, when he'd stroll in without a care in the world, his dirty fur and hunger proving that he had been out all day when I'd thought he was upstairs sleeping like a good boy.

One summer, when it felt as if the traffic on the road outside was even faster than usual, I decided to make a concerted effort to keep him in. However, it was so hot that I needed to open windows to let some air in. What was I going to do?

The stuffiest room seemed to be our bedroom. I thought that if I could get a little breeze in there during the day, Chris and I might have a better chance of sleeping at night. I went to the garden centre and got some pieces of trellis that I rigged up so the windows could be opened but Casper couldn't get near the small part that I worried he would squeeze through. I should have known he would see it as a challenge not a barrier. By the end of the first day, he had wiggled his way through somehow, jumped out of the window and onto the roof, leaped down onto the dustbins below and trotted across the road.

He always found a way to get out – he was such a little escape artist. Unless I fitted this cat with a tracking device, I would never be able to keep an eye on him twenty-four hours a day – even then, I bet he would have found a way to get round it. Casper didn't just enjoy being a wanderer, he seemed to need his freedom desperately. Perhaps it was a legacy from his life before us, but it was causing me more sleepless nights than ever.

CHAPTER 21

Who is Casper?

Casper's fame had brought new people to the fore. I'd had a few showing what I felt was too much interest in where I'd got Cassie. One day Edd rang me to say that something strange had happened. A man had called him to say that he believed Casper was his cat and he was, in effect, putting in a claim on him. He wanted to talk to me; he wanted to come and see Casper. Edd asked whether I was willing for him to give the man my phone number? What could I say?

I'd got Casper 'second-hand' and knew that he had a life before me; there had always been the chance that he had another family out there who would track him down one day. I remembered what had happened when the vet had discovered he was chipped all those years ago: the cat rescue lady had been desperate to ensure that Casper remained with me as she felt that he could not be returned to his previous home. Although she hadn't been able to give me any more details, there was an implication that he had been with someone who'd abused him. I would fight with every breath in my body to keep him from being returned to such an environment.

Minutes after I'd spoken to Edd, the man rang me. He seemed friendly and said that he, his wife and his two teenage children would like to come and see Casper – or 'Tom' as they called him. When they arrived, I was nervous, but Cassie showed absolutely no interest in them whatsoever. When they called him using the name they said they'd given him, he didn't prick up his ears.

I asked them why they thought he was theirs and how they'd lost him in the first place. The man informed me that they'd had 'Tom' for a few years and then got a kitten. Once the kitten was brought into the family, 'Tom' started spending most of his time with an old lady who lived nearby. When she moved, 'Tom' disappeared. I wondered why they'd left it all this time to track him down, but they were very evasive and couldn't even remember if he'd been chipped.

They didn't get down on the floor to play with Casper, they didn't hug him or seem relieved to have found him, which I would have expected if he had been the cat they'd lost all those years ago. They took lots of pictures as I asked again why they thought he was their cat. All they could come up with was that he had the same markings – black, white and brown.

This comment confirmed to me that they were making it all up. Casper would not have had brown splodges on him when he was younger; these were the equivalent of age spots that had appeared after years of lying in the sun. Strangely, they made no further attempts to claim Casper; they simply said 'goodbye' and left. I told Edd about it, but neither of us heard from them again, and I suspect they just wanted a day out to see the famous cat.

I took the opportunity to contact the chip people in order to try to find out a bit more about Casper's life before he'd come to me, but it was rather like dealing with an adoption agency. The whole process is shrouded in secrecy. All they would tell me was that he was originally called Danny and had been registered in Hampshire. It was very frustrating but I had to accept that I would never know the full story. Even after Casper died and I contacted them again, pleading for details and pointing out that surely privacy wasn't an issue now that he was gone, they refused to say anything.

I had my hands full with other matters too. In 2009, Jack started to deteriorate rapidly. He was one of Chris's favourites, but I knew that I would have to be the one to make the decision about whether it was his time to pass. He was getting thinner and thinner, because he was not eating properly and he was becoming weaker by the day. I'd been off work for some time with my own health problems but I knew that I would have to go back at some point soon. I was terribly worried about how Jack would cope while I was away. He was at the stage where he had to be helped in practically all of his day-to-day activities, such as being taken to his food dish or lifted into the litter tray.

One day, about a week or so before I was due to return to work, it was awfully cold and I couldn't find Jack anywhere. I went outside to look for him; although he was rarely venturing anywhere by that stage, I'd searched high and low inside with no luck. I opened the back door and there was the poor creature, huddled in the corner of the decking in the pouring rain. He wasn't attempting to find shelter; he looked like he'd given up. He was soaked through, completely bedraggled. 'Oh, Jack!' I cried, rushing over to lift him up and rush him indoors to the warmth. 'What are you up to, you silly old thing?'

I tried to convince myself that he'd been caught unexpectedly in a downpour, but I knew there was something seriously wrong. This was strange behaviour and I wondered whether his mind was going. It was almost as if he hadn't noticed it was raining, or as if he couldn't quite work out why he was so wet. As I dried him off with a towel and laid him by the fire to get warm, I gave him a gentle ticking off, more to appease myself than anything else. 'Now then,' I told him, 'we'll have no more of that silly behaviour. I think it best that you stay indoors where I can keep an eye on you.'

I tried to convince myself this was a one-off, but a few hours later he was missing again. I opened the back door straight away this time, and there he was. I had an old ceramic washbowl full of plants that I kept in the garden and it was overflowing with rainwater that day. Poor Jack was desperately trying to climb in. His legs had never worked properly and he was certainly far too weak to manage now, but he wouldn't give up. I knew that the decision had, in effect, been made for me. Just as I'd feared, his mind had gone.

Over the next few days, he kept wanting out, but I did my best to keep him inside. I was so scared that after I returned to work I would come home one day and he would have disappeared. What if I couldn't find him and he got trapped somewhere? I had to have him put down. It's the hardest decision in the world to make, but you have to get over it and do what's best for your pet. It was a stark reminder to me that in the midst of all the excitement over Casper life went on as normal and there were still pockets of sadness in it.

Things had calmed down a little with respect to Casper's fame when I got a call from Karen at First buses in the autumn. She said the company was launching a new type of bus and they were going to feature pictures of local people on the side panels. There would be a policeman, students, the dean of the university, all sorts of people – and they wanted Casper and me to be included. I was flattered but a bit worried at the thought of more pictures. Karen managed to convince me that it would be a nice gesture and a bit of fun; she said people were still asking about Casper and it would cement his position as one of Plymouth's most famous residents.

Everyone else had to go to into the main office to get their posters done, but Casper got special treatment, as always, and Karen came to my house to put together the images herself. I could hardly believe the size of them when I saw the finished product – they were quite literally the size of a bus. Casper and I were there for all to see, and we were chosen to launch the new vehicle.

This started off another round of publicity and, before I knew it, we were in women's magazines as well as newspapers. I started to get recognized a lot as I waited for the bus wherever I was, but people were always lovely to me.

The whole experience made me realize how many animal lovers there were out there. For so much of my life, I'd thought that no one else felt the same emotional pull as I did to other creatures, and there were times when I wondered if it was normal to get as upset as I did by cruelty to animals. My dream then, and now, would be to have a refuge of my own. If I won the lottery, I'd get a rambling farmhouse, a solid building surrounded by land, and I would take in anything that needed love and care – not just cats and dogs, but donkeys, birds, horses, all of God's creatures.

As I've grown older, I've become more vocal if I see people being cruel or thoughtless. I've also linked up with others who help animals, such as a donkey charity in Egypt called AWOL (Animal Welfare of Luxor, www.awol-egypt.org), which is run by an English couple, Pauline and Graham Warren. They try to re-educate Egyptians about the cruel practices they use, particularly the way they chain and tether their animals. Every night, this couple make soft webbing harnesses for the donkeys near Luxor. They visit those who use the cruellest chains and buckles, offering to trade them the soft, better quality items if they hand over the old-fashioned, evil implements. They also make reflective dog collars in small sizes. Sadly, dogs suffer dreadful neck wounds from being tied up with wire or sharp ropes. You can imagine the injuries caused. In the few years Pauline and Graham have been in Luxor, they have built up a rapport with the people and gained their respect. They also rescue dogs and cats and have quite a menagerie of their own. Their work is supported by donations from around the world. I do all I can to help their efforts. When we go over on holiday, we fill the case with as many medical supplies as we can: bandages, antiseptic creams etc. and anything to assist this couple in helping Egyptian animals. And lots of other things that they constantly need.

If you are visiting Luxor, please assist AWOL by taking any small amount of medical supplies and dog collars. This will assist this lovely, caring couple in helping to improve the safety and welfare of Egyptian animals. Contact them through their website.

I would urge everyone to be vigilant when they go abroad – don't simply accept things. If you see an animal being badly treated or beaten and you say nothing, you are contributing to its suffering. Most of these places depend on the tourist trade and if we all made it clear that we do not accept this type of behaviour, then maybe we can make a difference. I would have felt silly saying such things before Casper opened my eyes to the fact that there are so many people who feel the same as I do. Through Casper, I've found kindred spirits, good people who share my dream. Now I hope that we can shout with one voice to change things.

If there is anyone reading this who feels terrible loneliness, you should consider giving an abandoned cat a home. A cat will be the most loyal friend you could ever hope for. Whatever you give them, you will get back a hundredfold. You will never regret getting a cat – I certainly never did.

CHAPTER 22

Putting Plymouth on the Map

There were so many lovely aspects to what was going on with Casper that I had to laugh. When the original story had come out, I loved the line that said the drivers would count, 'Person, person, person, cat, person, person . . .' There were lots of puns in the newspapers about Casper's bus 'puss' and about the fact that he didn't have a Rover ticket.

The managing director of the bus company, Marc, says that he used to love coming into work and finding a stressful day punctuated by Casper stories. When he went to conferences and meetings, there was always someone who would bring up the subject of the cat who travelled on a First bus. He told me they got round the issue of whether Casper should have to pay (dogs do) by saying that in animal years he was a pensioner so he was entitled to free travel.

Like Rob, he thought someone was pulling his leg at first. He has a stressful job and here was someone wanting him to talk to the media about a cat who would only travel on a number three from his company – no wonder he was suspicious. As the stories of Casper did the rounds of the control office, he had to believe them. He'd been warned by Karen that there was about to be an explosion of interest in what was going on. Marc has since told me that he has heard stories of monkeys and parrots as assistance animals on public transport, so I suppose a bus-loving cat isn't too strange.

He wondered for a while if it was an urban myth, but once he'd accepted it, he started to wonder whether Casper might ride on his bus one day. This isn't as odd as it may sound, because in spite being in charge of the entire company, Marc still works as a driver sometimes. He was highly offended when he didn't receive the honour of Casper's patronage, but was soon distracted by friends and colleagues pulling his leg about how many awful puns he could squeeze in while doing interviews about Plymouth's favourite feline. There were plenty of mentions of 'furrs please, and 'cat-astrophic' happenings. Never one to miss a chance for some good product placement, the company line was that Casper obviously had good taste to choose only their buses and he appreciated the first class customer service – I couldn't disagree with any of that.

A little depot rivalry developed among the drivers, who would boast about how many times they'd had Casper on their bus. If a colleague hadn't been given that honour, they'd reflect on what good taste Casper had in choosing them.

Again, Marc reaffirmed my faith in British affection and humour. He told me that as long as Casper was causing no trouble and customers weren't complaining, there was absolutely no need to do anything to impede his journeys. They were only being human, he says, but I feel they went beyond the call of duty.

There are thirty-eight Plymouths in the world but my little cat put the English one on the map. People there had never experienced a local story becoming such a huge global phenomenon. Lots of drivers told me that they went home to their families at night and the first thing their children would ask them was: 'Did you have Casper on your bus today?' He was bringing families closer together. One chap told me that his wife and son hadn't shown any interest in his work for years, but all of a sudden they wanted him home in the hope that he could give them the latest update on the funny cat.

Marc's own little boy, Liam, although only a toddler, was starting to link what Daddy did with the cat on the bus. Rob, the driver who had done so much publicity with Casper, had two little girls, Caitlin and Libby, who saw their dad with him and were amazed. They suddenly believed that Daddy was famous and were desperate to meet the cat who was all over the news.

One day I got talking to a young teenage girl at the bus stop and asked her if she had ever seen Casper. 'No,' she replied, 'but my dad has had him on his bus.' Everyone knew Casper! I met her dad, Mike, a few days later and he told me that his five children and four grandchildren all knew about Cassie and they came together to hear stories about him. Mike had welcomed Casper on his bus on many occasions and seen him in the bus shelter even more often – well before the story came out. He says that cats do like bus shelters and he often sees them there, but he's never before come across one who actually got on the bus.

It put a smile on his face but I felt positively faint when he told me something that I'd never suspected: Casper apparently did not just do the number three circuit; he sometimes got off at the Square, crossed the road and got on another bus to Saltash. Mike joked that Cassie must have had something to do there, as he always seemed quite focused on his trip, but my blood ran cold. Just how far was this cat travelling and how many times was he facing danger every day? Mike has rescue cats and he knew that I was worried when I heard this, but there was nothing I could really do apart from cross my fingers every time my cat left the house.

Another bus driver was gaining a bit of celebrity status himself. Wookie is well known across Plymouth for his various props: the large foam hand he sticks out his window to give the thumbs up to any driver who lets him out, the deerstalker with ear flaps and peaked cap that he wears no matter what the weather and the bizarre green cuddly toy monkey he carries everywhere. Wookie took pictures of Casper and Monkey sharing a snack of chips together, and even posted photos of the two of them on Facebook. If ever anyone epitomized

British eccentricity, it was Wookie, and I feel that he and Casper would have got on brilliantly if Cassie ever decided to get on his bus. He considered it on many occasions, but perhaps thought that the luminous green monkey was too much competition.

I heard so many lovely tales from the drivers of how Casper was a wonderful talking point when they arrived home after a shift that my heart was full of pride at how much my little cat was achieving without doing very much. Our society is so fractured at times, and families feel such pressure with work and trying to juggle everything at once, that the happy topic of a cat on the bus brought some light relief and provided a common subject. It wasn't just the drivers and those at the depot who were experiencing this, but passengers too.

One gentleman contacted me some time after Casper's story first hit the papers. He wrote:

Dear Sue –
I have been reading the stories about your delightful cat with great interest. Some time ago, I lived in a small state in America where I worked as a teacher. When I moved there, a tiny ginger and white cat, not much bigger than a kitten, had been hanging around the school playground and the teachers weren't too sure what to do about it. The school I worked in was what we would probably now call one for those with learning difficulties – at the time, there was less concern for what to name things, but sometimes not as much concern as I would have liked for the children.

They loved to see this little cat, but there were two members of staff in particular who were adamant that she should be discouraged. The way in which there were so many arguments about this cat taught me more about the school politics than I could have learned in years. The head teacher had named the cat 'Betsy' after a cat she herself had loved as a child, and even the way that some teachers refused to call it by that name was a clear indication of how little they liked the head teacher herself rather than anything else. There was a standoff about Betsy the entire time I was at that school, which was almost four years. All I could see was that there were children with allergies, or who could not have a pet for other reasons, who lit up when they saw this little ginger thing run across to them. I could see that there were children who were so used to being frustrated by life, by the things they couldn't do, but who would brighten when they held her in their arms. They always managed to be gentle with her, and she always seemed to know just what they needed. I came back to the UK and never did find out the fate of Betsy, but, for some reason, when I read about Casper in the paper, he reminded me of her all those years ago. I would be willing to bet that your cat has given more love and more hope to people than you can possibly imagine. I now have three cats myself and I am constantly amazed by how they just seem to sense what we need – it seems as if Casper was very much a 'people cat' and I am sure that he would have cottoned on to what his fellow travellers needed.

Jim, Manchester

I wish I knew what had happened to Betsy too.

My cats had always shown tremendous compassion for us and for their fellow felines whenever they needed to, and I had no reason to suspect that Casper was any different. I was very proud of my cat for drawing families together and giving a little bit of comfort to people who saw him every day.

CHAPTER 23

Pulling Together

I knew from experience that cats can be a great source of comfort in times of need. The year before we got Casper, Chris had been feeling very unwell and we were pretty sure that he had kidney stones. He went to the doctor for some confirmation blood tests one morning before going to work. The results came through that evening, such was the urgency of what had been uncovered.

He was told to get home immediately and be at the haematology department of our local hospital the next afternoon. I couldn't understand why he would be sent there for kidney stones. We drove to the hospital in a haze. We were both pretty sure what was going on, as all of Chris's symptoms pointed to the diagnosis we felt sure he was going to receive. As soon as we arrived, he was taken in to the specialist, who didn't waste any time in telling us what was wrong.

'I'm sorry,' she said, 'there's no easy way to tell you this. You have leukaemia.'

When she spoke those words, I turned around and looked at the wall behind me. Who was she talking to, I wondered? It couldn't be us, could it? No, we were here because Chris had kidney stones. She needed to concentrate, I felt, get things right, make sure she had the correct notes. Leukaemia? That was cancer. Chris couldn't possibly have cancer, he just couldn't.

There was no one behind us and she *was* talking to my husband. It was his diagnosis and our world shattered around us the moment the consultant uttered those words. So many people have been in exactly the same position; I'm sure they've felt totally alone, just as we did. There were words floating around that no one wants applied to them or to someone they love – chronic myeloid, oncology, chemotherapy. All of these words are so loaded. When you hear them being said to the person you share your life with, it's like a bomb exploding. You wish that the clock could be turned back – not weeks or months but to that moment before you heard the word 'cancer'.

I'd worked in healthcare for years and I think I would have known what to say to someone else, but this was Chris. He was the man who had changed my life, who had made me happy and allowed me to be the person I had always wanted to be. He had seen me through my own health scares and had always been such a good person. Maybe everyone starts to think how unfair things are, and, of course, no one deserves cancer, but what had Chris ever done to harm anyone? We had been through so much over the years that it seemed an act of unspeakable cruelty to throw this at us too.

We had never considered cancer a possibility. We had come to hospital that day to find out about kidney stones. It turned out that when Chris had seen the GP (only the day before but it felt like a lifetime ago), his spleen had been three times the size it should have been, which is one of the first signs of this type of cancer. His white cell count was reading 150 when it should have been 5. If he hadn't gone to the doctor when he did, he would have been dead within six months. Now he had a fighting chance, but it would be far from plain sailing.

It was a terrible time. Chris had to get a bone marrow biopsy, which was a horrible process, a bone marrow harvest, constant blood tests. In fact, he had five bone marrow tests in one year. Initially he didn't respond to any of the chemotherapy treatment or injections, and his consultant sent him to a specialist in Hammersmith to look at the options. Things seemed very bleak but this man offered us one glimmer of hope. There was a course of treatment with a new drug that had been producing marvellous results in the US. However, it wasn't on the list of accepted medicines in this country. We were sent home with the information about it, aware that the consultant believed that this was really Chris's only option. If he couldn't get access to the drug, there was very little else that could be done.

Chris went back to his own consultant, who said that it was very unlikely that the local health authority would authorize a prescription. The drug cost over £17,000 a year and the budget simply wouldn't allow for it. I was furious but what could we do? 'Move to Scotland,' he said. 'They give it out like sweets up there. In the meantime, I'll write to the health authority and see what they say, but I really think there's very little chance. I'm so sorry.'

When Chris and I went home that night, it was difficult to be optimistic. His future was in the hands of faceless bureaucrats who would look at their balance sheets rather than the human cost of not authorizing the drug we now felt to be our only hope. I clung to what the doctor had said. I had no aversion to moving house; I'd done it plenty of times before, and this time it would be for a better reason than itchy feet. 'Why don't we move to Scotland?' I said to Chris. He had worked there many times and liked it, and I would do anything to increase his chances of surviving. We discussed it well into the night, and I would have been quite happy to start packing the next day, but Chris is more pragmatic and suggested we wait to see what the health authority said; perhaps they would surprise everyone.

They didn't. They refused the application.

The consultant was furious. He had done more research by this time and concurred completely with the Hammersmith doctor that this drug would give Chris the best chance. He went back to the health authority many times, pleading the case, making strong arguments, but they were difficult. In the end, he wrote the prescription anyway.

It was a miracle drug. Chris was in remission within a year and his case persuaded the authority to prescribe it much more freely when they saw the results. I was still so angry though. It infuriated me that my husband's health, his life, had been considered to be worth so little. If that drug had never been prescribed, he wouldn't be here today nor would all the other people who were given it as a result of his test case.

While Chris was terribly ill, the cats sensed something was going on. They became very gentle and watchful with him, and there always seemed to be one of our furry boys or girls sitting beside him when he was too weak to move or too sick from the treatment to get off the chair. While humans sometimes feel awkward or useless in the face of serious illness and the possibility of death, animals seem to take it in their stride, offering love and comfort in a simple way that does so much to help.

Ginny used to curl up beside him no matter how ill Chris was. She gave him such love, and even used to bring him presents of worms and baby frogs. There was never a mark on them, even though she used to carry them home in her mouth. She would deposit them in front of Chris as if she needed to give him something. Cats seem to need to do things for us just as we need to do things for them.

As Chris gradually got better, I felt that we had escaped. Perhaps now we could settle into a normal life, free of worry and concern. Casper's adventures brought joy to our days, and he managed, in some part, to tackle and negate the terrible negativity that I'd previously felt about humanity.

CHAPTER 24

Casper's Passing

It was 8.45a.m. on 14 January 2010 when I got the knock at my door that I'd always dreaded.

I was halfway through getting dressed when I heard the noise. It could have been anyone, I suppose – a delivery, some early post, a neighbour. But I knew. I just knew, as I walked down the stairs, that as soon as I opened the door, the rug would be pulled out from under me. Do we have some sort of sixth sense when bad things, awful things, are about to affect our lives? Not always – there can be a phone call in the middle of the night that we never expected or a letter that contains information that will change our lives, and they are bolts from the blue. However, I've always had feelings about things – premonitions and senses. On this day I desperately wanted to be wrong, but a sense of foreboding warned me against opening the door, told me not to listen to whatever the person on the other side had to say. Sadly, I had no choice. I had to open the door.

Waiting for me on the other side was a lady I vaguely knew. She lived in the same street and I often saw her walking past with her little girl. We had said 'hello' and exchanged a few words about Casper from time to time, and she was always friendly and interested in what he was up to. That day she was as white as a ghost and shaking.

'I'm so sorry,' she said. 'I'm not sure how to tell you this but . . . it's Casper. He's been hit.'

I listened to the words but they were no surprise to me. Since the moment I'd heard the doorbell, I'd known this was it. This was the moment when all my worst nightmares were about to come true. I felt as if the woman's voice was coming through a tunnel as she continued to tell me what had happened. It came to me in fragments . . .

There was a car . . . a taxi . . .

Going too fast . . . speeding . . .

If he had crossed the road a moment earlier or a moment later . . . he didn't stand a chance . . .

I heard a bang . . . Casper . . . Casper . . .

The woman said that she'd been walking along Poole Park Road when she was aware of a vehicle driving up behind her. She heard a bang so loud that she'd turned around. She realized that the private hire taxi was driving along at such a rate that she needed to push her little girl off the pavement onto a grass verge, as she thought the car might hit the toddler. The taxi sped past, not slowing down in the slightest. She checked that her child was all right, then looked back again to see what had caused the bang.

It was Casper.

She had heard Casper being hit.

I grabbed a coat to put over my nightdress, vaguely aware that she was still talking. 'He was hit,' she said, 'but he's still alive. I saw him crawl across the road, Sue. Maybe he's OK?' There was desperation in her voice and panic in my heart. I raced out the door, past the woman who was still standing there with her little girl, both of them quiet, both of them waiting to see whether Casper was safe.

The woman called, 'I think he's under a parked car,' just as I realized the same thing myself. He was. Casper was there! In a neighbour's driveway, under their car, he was hiding. Shivering and terrified, I scooped him up in my arms and hurried back inside. 'Thank you,' I whispered to the woman as I went in.

Casper was alive but only just.

My darling cat wasn't making any noise. I laid him on the sofa with a blanket over him as I flew upstairs to grab some clothes. I needed to get him to the vet immediately. As I put on the first things I could find, I tried to put the image of Casper out of my mind and focus on the fact that he was here with me, and I would do everything in my power to save him. I'd never let that dear cat out of my sight again. I'd lock doors, seal windows; I'd move a hundred miles away into the heart of the country if I needed to. I made all of these promises in my head, but it was a desperate ploy to try to block out the image I'd had when I picked him up. His back end had been swinging as if he had no control over it whatsoever and I feared with every part of my body and soul that his back had been broken. Vets can do wonders, I muttered. Vets can work miracles. I knew time was against me and I needed to get a taxi, get to the vet, get things in motion to try to reverse the awful thing that had just happened.

I was away from Cassie for less than a minute, but somehow, in my absence and despite his horrific injuries, he had managed to get off the sofa and was now lying by the door.

Everything seemed to slow down.

I'd been in such a rush, such a panic, but now I felt as if the clocks had stopped. My wonderful Casper was taking his last breaths. I just knew it. I needed no medical expertise, no veterinary education. This was it. This was the end.

I lay down on the floor beside him and stroked him constantly. I don't know whether he was conscious or not, but I needed to whisper words of comfort for both of us.

What did I say? I don't know.

What did I feel? During those final moments, I'm not sure.

Together, in love, I held my boy as he left this world.

The pain was almost unbearable, but not being there with Casper as he breathed his last would have been more than I could have endured. I was honoured to be there, even if my heart was breaking. And it was. It truly was.

CHAPTER 25

The Hardest Days

I had to do something. There was no doubt in my mind that Cassie had gone, but there were still things that I had to do for him. I didn't want to see him lying on the floor, shattered and empty, a shadow of the wonderful cat he had been. I knew that I had to get him to the vet, where he would be treated with dignity.

I picked up my gorgeous cat and wrapped him in a blanket. My hands seemed to belong to someone else and I fumbled desperately as I tried to swaddle him. It was important to me that he was treated with love and care from this moment on, and I tried to be so gentle with his poor broken shell.

I knew that the vet's phone line had been broken for almost a week and time was against me. They closed at 10a.m., which meant I had only fifteen minutes to get there. I rang the animal hospital on the other side of Plymouth and asked if they could call my vet, tell them that Casper had been hit and that I needed to bring him in. I had a horrible feeling that if they didn't know in advance, I'd be faced with locked doors when I arrived.

By the time I got there, it was after ten, but they were waiting for me. The receptionist was very fond of Cassie, and had read about him in the newspapers, so she was terribly upset. The rest of that visit is a bit of a blur. I knew he was dead; I didn't need anyone to confirm it for me. Perhaps I just had to do something to make it real. By going to the vet, I was completing my commitment to Casper by ensuring that, until his last moment, he would be cared for. Maybe I also needed to say the words out loud – *Casper is dead*.

There were no more words to say to Casper. I kissed him and sent him all my love and then I left him. I didn't turn back; I didn't run to his side a hundred times. He was gone. He wasn't Cassie any more, and there was nothing I could do about it.

Chris had been away since just after Christmas, but was due home that night. I called him, in floods of tears, to let him know what had happened, and felt that I had to hold on until he got back. I spent the rest of the morning crying, and that was how it should be. Carrying on as if nothing had happened, going about life as if it wasn't the darkest of days – how could I have pretended?

A picture of what had happened to Casper kept emerging through the tears. The lady with the toddler told me that the bang was so loud she'd heard it clearly and turned around in fear. The driver must have heard it too; he must have felt it. Why didn't he stop? He must have known that he'd hit something. Didn't he care? What if he thought nothing had happened and he continued to drive like that? What if next time it was a child?

Despite my grief, I could not, in all conscience, allow this to go unchallenged. I rang the police and told them what had happened. They informed me that there is no legal requirement for a driver to stop if they hit a cat, whereas with a dog they must do so. This seemed terribly unfair to me, but I expressed my concern that the driver was unsafe and that he could cause injury or worse if allowed to go unchecked. The policewoman was sympathetic but said there was nothing that could be done – dangerous driving required two witnesses and it would have to be those witnesses who made the complaint.

I lay down, my head full of the injustice of it all, my heart heavy with loss. I felt so alone. Then, as if someone had sent me a message, I realized that I was *not* alone. People cared. People loved Casper. They needed to know that he was gone, and I had a duty to tell them. My first call was to Edd at the *Plymouth Herald.* The words were so difficult to say, but the fact that he was shocked, sympathetic and emotional about it too made me realize this was the right decision. Casper had spent so long in the public eye that those who had rejoiced in his adventures had a right to know what had happened. I realized at that moment that Casper didn't just belong to me, he belonged to everyone.

Edd's immediate response was to tell me that he would put something in the paper as soon as possible to inform readers. I knew there was also someone else I had to contact immediately – Rob. By this time of day, the bus drivers on the number three would be starting to look for Casper, wondering whether he'd be in the bus shelter yet or taking their route that day. It made me terribly sad to think that they, too, were ignorant of what had happened and that they would never see him again.

With a shaking hand and a lump in my throat, I rang Rob. 'Hi Sue,' he said, cheery as always, 'what can I do for you today?' The story poured out of me, as I asked him to tell Karen and the others. I could tell that he was in shock too, but he was practical and said he would let everyone know. He urged me to take care of myself.

I settled back onto the sofa, without a clue as to what I should do next. I'd called the people who had been most involved in Casper's public world. As I lay there, I knew that they would be telling others, while I faced the reality of life without him on my own.

The house was empty of Casper but today he wasn't wandering, he wasn't waiting on the bus, he wasn't sitting under the hedge, watching dogs. He was gone and there was nothing I could do to bring him back. Every time I felt my mind wander, I tried to stop it. There was no benefit in thinking about how he'd looked when I picked him up from under the car, or lain him on the sofa, or saw him at the door, or left him with the vet. That was in the past and I would only hurt more if I dwelt on it.

As I sat there, alone and lost, I had no idea that the news of Casper's death had had an immediate impact. Rob had put up a notice in the bus depot. It echoed those from earlier times, but today it contained a much sadder message.

CASPER THE CAT HAS DIED

I HAVE THIS MORNING BEEN MADE AWARE OF
THE SAD NEWS THAT CASPER THE CAT HAS
DIED. A CAR HIT HIM AND, UNFORTUNATELY,
BY THE TIME HIS OWNER GOT TO HIM
HIS INJURIES WERE NOT SURVIVABLE. HIS
OWNER, SUE, HAS ASKED ME TO PASS ON HER
HEARTFELT THANKS TO ALL OF THOSE WHO
LOOKED AFTER HIM WHEN ON THE BUS AND
EVERYONE WHO HAS ASKED AFTER HIM.

MANY THANKS – ROB

One driver, Jo, later told me that there was complete shock in the depot. People had got so used to Casper and his funny little ways; they considered him one of their own, and now he was gone. It was, of course, something that we'd all worried about ever since we'd found out about his habit of crossing the road and wandering about. As time had gone on, perhaps some of his friends had thought he was a remarkable cat in more ways than one; maybe he would avoid the inevitable and survive the traffic. I must confess that I'd never thought this way; I'd always worried, I'd always thought this day would come.

The hours passed slowly until Chris came home. I heard the car pull up outside and knew what he would be feeling – the absolute emptiness that Casper was not there to run to him. I fell into his arms with all the sadness of the day's events pouring out of me. It felt so real. It felt so final.

CHAPTER 26

RIP Casper

Edd was true to his word. Within a few days, the story of Casper's death was in the *Plymouth Herald*.

Celebrity cat killed in hit and run

A much-loved Barne Barton cat who made headlines around the world has died after being hit by a car.

Casper the commuting cat fast became a celebrity on Plymouth buses when he used to politely queue with the other passengers, before hopping aboard to travel around the city.

His owner says she's devastated and doubts she'll ever have a cat like Casper again.

Sue Finden said: 'I never dreamt I'd miss an animal as much as I miss him. He was lovely and loved people so much — he was such a different character.'

She said she only found out about his death when a woman knocked on her door to tell her she'd seen Casper get hit by a car, but the driver hadn't stopped.

She took Casper into the house but realized he'd already died.

'If he'd been ill we might have prepared for it but it hasn't helped us that the driver didn't stop – we couldn't believe it.'

Sue discovered Casper's escapades when he followed her onto a bus and a First Devon and Cornwall bus driver said he travelled with them all the time.

The Plymouth puss featured on websites from England's tabloids to the USA's mystateline.com.

Headlines Casper enjoyed included 'Stowaway Cat gets bus-ted', in The Sun while The Press Association went with 'Joyrider Casper given a puss pass'. He also appeared on a diverse range of other websites.

He proved a hit with drivers and customers alike, who always made sure he returned home safely.

Casper's journey took him from just outside his house in Poole Park Road to the final stop at Royal Parade and back, via St Budeaux Square, HMS Drake, Keyham, Devonport and Stonehouse.

Mrs Finden added: 'I thought it was only decent that I let the public know what had happened to him as he made so many friends and would turn up to the bus stop like clockwork.'

She posted a notice at Casper's usual bus stop in Poole Park Road, saying: 'Many local people knew Casper, who loved everyone. He also enjoyed the bus journeys.

'Sadly a motorist hit him . . . and did not stop.

'Casper died from his injuries. He will be greatly missed . . . he was a much loved pet who had so much character. Thank you to all those who befriended him.'

Marc Reddy, Managing Director of First Devon and Cornwall, expressed the company's sympathy for the friendly feline.

He said: 'We were devastated to hear that Casper had been involved in an accident; he was a regular passenger on Service 3 in Plymouth and had become very well known across the business.

'On hearing the news of his death, many of the drivers expressed sympathy for him and Susan, and we contacted her to offer our collective condolences.

'Casper touched many people's lives and clearly had a very exciting life – travelling around Plymouth and who knows where else. I suspect he's now exploring heaven and is telling all the other cats up there about the many adventures he had.'

Casper was so popular that an image of him was emblazoned onto the side of a First Devon and Cornwall bus.

Mr Reddy said: 'Casper's image will remain on the bus for some time to come, and we hope that seeing it around town will give Susan some comfort.'

He added that Casper is also due to feature in a children's TV programme later this year, detailing his exploits on the bus in the city.

'His memory will live on, giving people pleasure, for a while yet,' he added.

Mrs Finden said that Casper had been cremated at a local vet's crematorium. She would like to thank the woman who let her know that Casper had been hit.

As Ed mentioned, I had decided to put up a notice in the bus shelter with a picture of Casper so that all his fellow passengers would know that he would no longer be taking any trips with them. I wrote:

Many local people knew Casper who loved everyone and his trips on the bus. Sadly, a motorist hit him at about 8.45a.m. on Thursday, 14 January, and did not stop. Casper died from his injuries. He will be greatly missed by many, but especially by us, as he was a very much loved pet who had so much character. Thank you to all who befriended him.

The news of Casper's sad end was spreading quickly. Newspapers were picking up on Edd's report and tributes started flooding into Facebook from all over the world after a Casper page was set up. It was staggering. There was such an outpouring of affection and grief. So many people were reaching out to me even though I had no idea who they were. I was extremely touched, but also very emotional every time I read the kind words.

Casper was a legend amongst felines across the globe. Truly wish I could have sat next to you on the bus. Deepest sympathies to your owner, your friends at First bus and everyone else's heart you touched. I also hope the rotters

who knocked you over and didn't bother to stop and help are found and they get their just desserts. Sweet dreams little kitty.
Vix

Poor kitty, he brought a great smile to my face reading about his travels.
Kev

What a tragedy. Deep condolences to Susan, the bus company and its wonderful and caring drivers, as well as the passengers who had had the wonderful opportunity to share their rides with such a special and smart feline. Rest in peace Casper, we all love you!
Noni

It is truly amazing that this cat can even touch hearts across the pond. RIP Casper. You were a very special cat.
Chris

I am saddened to hear the tragic news of what has happened to poor Casper – whoever did this to him wants locking up with the key thrown away. To leave him dying and not stop to help is appalling, let's hope divine retribution kicks in and they soon get their comeuppance, that was a heartless act of extreme merciless cruelty against a poor defenceless animal. Shame on the evil culprit. As a cat lover who also has a cat of real character I was totally devastated when someone did this twice to my cat. Thankfully she was found in time and

saved but I really feel for Casper and his owners. RIP Casper and sincerest condolences to all who knew and loved Casper. Let's hope Casper has gone on to ride the astral buses in the world beyond, forever travelling, safe and happy.
Evelyn

RIP Casper – have a safe journey to heaven.
David

Terrible to lose a pet. It's as bad as losing a family member because that's what they are.
Sarah

It's not like running over some random cat, it's like running over a person!
Matt

Here I was thinking people DISLIKE commuting! Now this cat comes in and turns my world upside down. I will never forget him.
Thomas

Soooooo sad! When I first read about Casper, it made me laugh so much, bless his little feline soul. RIP Casper and love to his family.
Emma

Heartbroken to read the news. How could somebody be so cruel as to drive on without stopping? A big 'thank

you' to all those kind First bus drivers in Plymouth who looked after him on his daily journey. Perhaps somebody in Plymouth could put some flowers at Casper's stop for us all?
Paul

I'm gutted that I didn't ever catch the same bus as Casper! The coolest cat ever!
Annie

I was extremely saddened to learn about the death of this beautiful and unique cat. I first learned about Casper from a feature article in a magazine, which detailed his daily travels by bus, and I enjoyed reading about his adventures. Now if I ever go to England, I'll never have the chance to ride on the same bus — he was truly one of a kind. My deepest sympathies go out to his owner as well as his many friends who knew and loved him.
Michelle

The comments went on and on. So many people had read about Casper and so many people were grieving. They felt the loss too. Commentators often say that as the world gets smaller through technology, we're losing our sense of neighbourliness and contact with others. This may indeed be the case in some instances, but I found that, through the Internet, I had thousands of friends I never knew existed. When I needed to dwell on the space Casper had left in my world, all I had to do was log on and there were comments from new people who wanted to reach out and offer me words of condolence. Again, Casper had achieved something incredible.

The story was covered in all the British national newspapers and I received personal letters from editors and journalists across the country. As the days passed, the global phenomenon that was Casper gained pace, but I felt cheated. Many of the tributes were so beautiful, but I wished they had not been necessary. Casper had been snatched from us so unfairly and so quickly. If he'd been ill, maybe I would have been more prepared for his death. I was always hurt by the loss of any of my cats, but Casper was such an amazing boy that his death hit me hard. I knew that the interest would fade and I would be left with my memories. Casper had blessed me with so many beautiful ones, and I was desperately trying to hold onto that, but the pain was raw and I didn't know how I was going to cope in the future without him.

CHAPTER 27

Discovering the Rainbow Bridge

People tried to be kind, but I didn't know what to say to them. Many asked what had happened to Cassie, and I couldn't understand what they meant for a while. He'd died. He'd been killed. What else was there to say? But then I realized that they were asking what had happened to what was left of him – to his remains, I suppose. As I've already explained, I never bury my cats in the garden because I would hate for them to be left alone when I move. Some enquired whether I'd kept Casper's ashes. I categorically had not. All of my pets are treated the same way when they leave my life. Casper was special, but I wasn't going to favour him over any of the others. The only thing that soothes me is the hope that they are all together in Heaven.

I have to take such salves wherever I find them, or the hurt would never go away. Very soon after Casper died, I heard of the rainbow bridge for the first time. When there has been a particularly close connection between an animal and a person, the animal crosses the rainbow bridge to wait for the person when they pass over. One website describes it beautifully, although sadly they say that the author of these words is unknown. I'd love to tell them how helpful these lines are.

Just this side of heaven is a place called Rainbow Bridge.

When an animal dies that has been especially close to someone here, that pet goes to Rainbow Bridge.

There are meadows and hills for all of our special friends so they can run and play together.

There is plenty of food, water and sunshine, and our friends are warm and comfortable.

All the animals who had been ill and old are restored to health and vigour; those who were hurt or maimed are made whole and strong again, just as we remember them in our dreams of days and times gone by.

The animals are happy and content, except for one small thing; they each miss someone very special to them, who had to be left behind.

They all run and play together, but the day comes when one suddenly stops and looks into the distance. His bright eyes are intent; his eager body quivers. Suddenly he begins to run from the group, flying over the green grass, his legs carrying him faster and faster.

You have been spotted, and when you and your special friend finally meet, you cling together in joyous reunion, never to be parted again. The happy kisses rain upon your face; your hands again caress the beloved head, and you

look once more into the trusting eyes of your pet, so long
gone from your life but never absent from your heart.
Then you cross Rainbow Bridge together . . .

Some of the newspaper stories about Casper's death
commented on this idea and my closest friend, Alice, in
Cumbria sent me an email explaining the whole concept.
The more I think of it, the more it makes sense. I smile
when I think of those waiting for me – there will be a
stampede, given all the animals I've had over the years!

I don't automatically believe in things like that. I like
to have things proven to me beyond doubt, but something happened over twenty years ago that removed
some of my cynicism. I've returned to the memory of
it many times since Casper's death, as it is the closest to
proof of an afterlife I have ever come across.

In 1987, my son Greg was in a horrendous car crash.
He wasn't expected to survive – in fact, I was asked for
permission to donate his kidneys, as it was assumed
he would die very soon. He'd never been christened
as a child, and this bothered me. My relationship with
his father had been so bad that it had simply never
happened. Now that he was facing the worst prognosis,
I was suddenly stricken with panic that the blessing had
never taken place. Greg was on life support for a week,
and during this time Chris and I arranged for the chris-
tening to take place.

After the service, things still looked bleak and the
doctors said that Greg would be taken off the life support

machine to see which way it went. Everything was very negative. I was told that when the body closes down, the last thing to go is hearing so I was encouraged to talk and reassure him constantly. Incredibly, Greg rallied and began his long journey to recovery. The trauma he had suffered was awful. Although we were delighted he had survived, he became terribly violent. He attacked me on a number of occasions, although I don't think he even knew who I was when it happened. He broke my teeth on one visit. He was so unpredictable that he ended up being cared for in an Army hospital by soldiers, even although he wasn't in the Services himself.

I was terrified of my own child. Greg was such a big chap anyway, covered in tattoos and much taller than me. I was with him as much as I possibly could be but I must admit that I started to dread the times I was with him as I never knew what would happen. He got to the stage where little could be done for him: he had hip problems, damage to his back, a fractured skull and so much more. He was placed in a psychiatric unit and I honestly thought that would be the end of him. Greg was surrounded by people who were suicide risks and I felt it was only a matter of time before he would be influenced by them. Chris and I were trying to make his life worth living, but we were fighting a losing battle.

One morning, I approached Greg's bed with a heavy heart only to be greeted by the sight of him sitting up with a smile on his face. 'Hi Mum,' he grinned. 'I've got something to tell you.' I was shocked; he'd changed overnight.

'What's happened?' I asked. 'What's going on?'

Greg told me that it was time for things to get back on track and he'd remembered what his grandma had said to him. His grandma, I wondered? She'd been dead for a year.

'I saw her, you know,' he said to me. 'I saw my grandma.'

'Did you, love?' I replied gently, playing along.

Greg laughed softly. 'I'm not mad. I know she's dead, but I saw her when I was in hospital.'

'When was this?'

'Back when they took me off the life support machine,' he answered. 'I was walking along a tunnel with a bright light when I saw her. I thought she was waiting for me, but she wasn't. She told me to go; she said it wasn't time. I did as I was told, Mum. I came back.'

We've never spoken about it since. I was so relieved that Greg was back to some semblance of normality and that the dark days were over. He has had a terrible time since then, trying to build his body and his life back up again, but that day on the psychiatric ward I saw a complete transformation and I believe that was because he remembered the miracle that had happened. Greg isn't the sort of person who believes in angels and spirits, and that, in itself, made me think it must be true. I think I've always been almost scared of truly believing in such things.

I didn't want to accept that Cassie was dead. I am open to the possibility that there is more to this world than we know, and I would be delighted if Casper could prove that to me. I've heard that some people believe that if an animal dies unexpectedly – meaning they weren't expecting it to happen – then their soul gets 'stuck'. They can't move on until they accept that they are no longer in this world. When they do finally accept it, strange things can happen. I've heard of people who suddenly acquire a cat with no intention of doing so, as it somehow reminds them of the one they have lost. Or they look at a dozen rescue pets, feel none is right, then one little creature turns up on their doorstep and it's as if the decision has been taken out of their hands. I wonder whether a part of the soul of that other cat is with them? Have they been sent to look after the bereaved owner? A hundred questions like that go through my mind. Some days I take comfort in them; other days I give myself a telling off for thinking such nonsense. Only time will tell whether I will receive any sort of message from Casper, but I hope I do.

I did look for signs and messages. On the day that Casper died, there was a story in one of the papers about some poor cats who'd been terribly abused. Casper's tale was on one side of the paper, and on the other there was a shocking report of one hundred Persian kittens who'd been discovered and rescued by animal welfare officers. They were in such a terrible state from the poor care they'd received that they had to be shaved to remove the urine burns.

I couldn't get those kittens out of my mind. As the days passed after Cassie's death, I wondered whether this was a sign. Was I being told by someone – something? – that I needed to open my home to one of these poor damaged little animals? Chris told me that if I wanted to get one, I should, but I was torn. It was too soon; it wasn't time. Casper had only just gone. And yet, and yet . . .

I felt there was a link. I couldn't settle. I went to the local cat rescue centre and asked what the procedure was for adopting a cat. The woman said there were forms to complete and I'd need a home visit. She then asked if I'd been a cat owner previously. All my good intentions about keeping quiet about Casper were broken in an instant. It all poured out of me and I was terribly upset. The lady said she couldn't risk the same thing happening to another cat, and I should consider a house pet. At that point, I informed her that I knew exactly what sort of cat I wanted to give a home to – one of the abused Persian kittens I'd seen in the paper. She said I was too late.

'That happened months ago, but the papers are only picking up on it now. We had sixteen of them – two died because of what had been done to them, but the others have all been re-homed to loving families.'

She asked me whether I'd like to look at the other cats they had, but I couldn't. I still felt that the link was with the Persians because they had shared headlines with Casper.

I went home and still couldn't settle. If the local cat rescue centre had known the fate of sixteen of the kittens that meant another eighty-four were out there. I spent the next few days searching the Internet, contacting rescue centres all over the country, chasing up comments on websites – all to no avail. Most of the kittens had been re-homed, and some seemed to have just disappeared. I had to accept that this simply wasn't meant to be. I'd spent a lot of time and energy on what had amounted to a wild goose (or kitten) chase.

Perhaps it was my way of getting through those difficult early days without Casper, or perhaps I really did think there was a message waiting for me. Who knows? Whatever the reason, whatever the answer, I wasn't going to be given the privilege of looking after one of those poor kittens, so I would have to channel my love elsewhere.

CHAPTER 28

Filling the Gap

It didn't take long for people to start offering me 'new' cats. I'm sure that many of them meant well, but there was no way I could bring another cat into my life within days of Casper dying. It wouldn't have been fair on the new arrival, as I was still grieving, and I would have felt I was betraying Casper. He couldn't be replaced so quickly or easily – no cat could. They're all individuals with their own characters.

Apart from that, I was also left with a terrible fear of the road. I'd always worried that Casper would be run over as he went about his daily adventures, but now the worst had happened, what was to stop another cat being killed? Although I have loved all my cats dearly and would never have been without the experience each of them has brought me, I can't deny that every loss takes a little piece of my heart. We all have an enormous capacity to love, but losing so many beautiful animals has made me realize just how high the emotional cost is.

I'm not alone in thinking this, of course. As the letters and messages started to pour in from around the world, I quickly recognized that loss knows no geographical boundaries. Many people told me about their pets, but one young girl really touched me with her story of those she had loved and who had sadly passed on.

Dear Sue –

I hope that you don't mind me writing to you at a time when you are probably still very upset about Casper. When I was six, me and my little brother went to a cat rescue centre and got three kittens. They were all so beautiful – although they were very different from each other, they were from the same family. Molly was tiny and like grey velvet, Freddie was much bigger with grey and white stripes, and Oscar was a tabby. They all had really different personalities too – when we got them all home, they were too small to climb the stairs, but they soon got really naughty and Oscar would take a running leap from one end of the room to the other and claw his way up my mum's back! Freddie liked to make holes underneath the sofas for them all to hide, but Molly was the one I loved most. She chattered away all the time and we used to pretend she was moaning about things. She was such a dainty little lady, about half the size of her brothers, and she would disappear for ages, only coming back when she felt like it, with lots of complaining to do – and sometimes smelling of perfume! We wondered where she went and whether she had another life somewhere.

As I got older, I told her all my worries – when I was bullied at school, when a teacher hit me, when my mum was ill. When she didn't come back one day, we weren't too worried as she did like disappearing, but the days started to add up and it was soon a week since she had been home. It didn't feel right and I tried to make myself strong, thinking I would never see her again. I was right. I came home from school one day and my mum told me that my gran had found Molly's body close to a main road. It seemed that she had been hit by a lorry. My dad carried her home and I thought my heart would break. I couldn't believe that I'd never see her again, that I hadn't say 'goodbye', that I hadn't realized she was going to die. I just wanted to hold her one last time.

I missed her so much, and I vowed to love Oscar and Freddie even more. We moved house a few years later and the boys went to stay with my grandparents until we settled in. Although we were moving to the country with hills out our back door, and the North Sea and beach out the front, there was also a busy road. Freddie and Oscar stayed with my gran and grandad for a while as we built our new house – I wished they had stayed there forever, because within weeks of coming back to us, Freddie was run over. I couldn't believe it had happened again, and all the hurt I had felt with Molly came back.

We then got two kittens to keep Oscar company – Trixie and Lola. Although they were feral, they liked to stay at home, and I was so glad. Oscar did go out, and my heart was in my mouth every morning wondering whether he would make it *home, so I was glad that the girls were safe. It turned out that they weren't as safe as I'd hoped. When she was only eight months old, Trixie started to get very sick. She was crying in pain and unable to eat. We took her to the vet who said that there was a lump in her stomach, which felt as though she had swallowed something, but that she was too weak for an operation. She was put on a drip until she got stronger and when they did open her up, found that she had swallowed an ear plug. She never recovered and there was so much internal damage that she had to be put to sleep. I felt so angry – why did some people manage to keep their pets for so long when ours kept dying? We were good people, we gave them loving homes and were always kind, so why did this keep happening?*

All of the losses had been too much, so we got a dog in the hope that we could have more control. Jojo was the most beautiful Weimaraner – he wasn't very clever though, and he fell madly in love with Lola despite the fact that she spent most of her time hitting him! He didn't seem to mind and would just gaze at her as she would lazily lie there just slapping him over and over! She was very like Molly and I felt very close to her. When mum took Jojo for a walk up into the hills, Lola would often trot along behind them the whole way, and when she came back for an exhausted sleep, Jojo would just stare at her lovingly! I finally felt that things were working out with our pets, and as we packed for Christmas in Florida, was happy that the cats were going to a woman we knew, and Jojo was going to stay with his mum and sister. I don't know what it was, but when there was a knock at our door, my heart sank. It was almost as if

I had been too happy – where was Jojo? There was a man there, talking to my dad, and I knew something was wrong. Jojo had got out and been hit by a car. All of these cats and now our dog; I didn't know if I could cope with losing one after the other and I felt that I didn't want to.

It sounds awful, but, after that, I felt as if I was just waiting for something to happen to Lola or Oscar. A few months later, when I went out to wait on the bus to high school, I looked across the road and saw a ball of fur, long hair, black and white. I just knew it was her, I just knew it was Lola. She had only started going out at night since Jojo had died, and, as I ran inside crying, I felt as if this was always going to happen. We still have Oscar and I love him so much, but I want him to stay inside all the time, which probably isn't fair for a cat. I don't want any more pets ever. It hurts too much. You give them all your love, tell them all your secrets, then someone is so thoughtless, so heartless, that they run them over without thinking just how much they are tearing a family apart.

Cats are so independent and I wonder whether we just have to pay a price for having them in our lives. They go away and do things we know nothing about, but, for all we know, they could be facing danger constantly. Although I want to love another cat, I feel as if I can't risk it – there are only so many times I can have my heart broken. I know that you will always miss Casper and I hope that it doesn't hurt so much after a while – the pain never goes away, but sometimes you can manage to forget.

Evie, 14, Aberdeenshire

This letter made me cry so much – there was such a lot of pain in it. It was written by a girl who obviously loved her pets enormously but who was having to face up to the hard facts of losing them, one after another.

I knew exactly what she meant when she said that it seemed so unfair that some people managed to keep their pets for years despite not really loving or looking after them. I've seen animals treated with such cruelty but they still love their owners, still hope for a bit of kindness, and those owners don't seem to realize how blessed they are to have those creatures in their lives. Yet here was this poor young girl facing up to the loss of so many in such a short time. If people could only see that they are privileged to have animals in their lives and make the most of them when they are there. Many of us would do anything to have a few more moments with the ones who continue to hold our hearts even though they have passed on.

I try to reply to everyone who gets in touch about Casper, but this was a tricky one. I told this young girl that I really appreciated her taking the time to write and share her thoughts, but that I was sad reading about her pain. I wished that I could give her a simple reason why God takes our cherished pets away so suddenly, but I couldn't. I suppose He has the answer, but whatever that reason may be, it still seems terribly unfair.

What Evie's letter brought home to me was that, although my heart was breaking over the loss of Casper, the thought of her losing so many pets at such a young age, one after the other in such horrible circumstances, was horrible. I pleaded with her:

> *Please don't say you will never have another pet. Maybe one day, somewhere, somehow, an animal will cross your path and you will feel that you can give it a loving home. You may have to wait until you are older, but you will know when the time is right. You love animals too much to say 'never again'.*

Her hurt sounded so deep. I recognized that she was afraid of loving a new pet if it was going to be ripped away too soon. But this young girl had hit the nail on the head: we do indeed pay a high price for having animals in our lives. Of the eight cats Chris and I had in our lives not so long ago, we now had two and each loss had taken something from my heart. Each time I vowed that I would never be able to go through it again, but I couldn't be without cats in my life. I feel it is my purpose to give happy, loving homes to poor old things with little hope left and, if in the process I have to go through some hurt myself, that's just the way it has to be. I couldn't have a home without my babies. We were all put here for a reason and perhaps this is mine. I finished by telling her:

> *Your letter will always be treasured, Evie, and I will keep it forever as it was from your heart. As I said before, the hurt never ever goes and we don't forget the pets we love, but*

somehow we do learn to adapt and loving is what many of us do best.

I hope my words comforted her in some small way, as hers had touched me. These people who were taking their time to contact me were managing to fill the gap left by Casper in a truly amazing way – the human kindness that was being sent to me in floods was changing the way I thought of the world, and I could take enormous comfort in that.

CHAPTER 29

The Kindness of Strangers

I had some decisions to make. The first was whether I wanted to see the photograph of Casper and me on the buses every day. Karen from First Devon and Cornwall had been very solicitous and worried that it might be too much emotionally. Despite the cost and the inconvenience, she reassured me that the company would comply totally with whatever I wanted. If I couldn't bear to see Casper in happier times, then they would remove the posters immediately. I thought it over and did have worries that I might have to face some horrid comments if the images remained. However, the longer I considered it, the more I felt that it was perhaps a fitting tribute to Casper. He had loved those buses so much and the photos were delightful ones, so I decided to allow them to remain. I have had only lovely comments from fellow passengers. I still get a shock at times when I see them, but there are such happy memories associated with those days too.

The other decision I had to make was in relation to the driver who had killed Casper. As I've said, there is no law that requires someone in charge of a vehicle to report any accident with a cat, but I continued to be angered at the unfairness of this situation. If the driver had turned up at my door, I would have been upset, but if he had come to apologize, then I believe it would have made a difference and helped me to find closure. I couldn't help but think that he had 'got away with it' – perhaps it wasn't his first time, perhaps more families had been decimated by his carelessness. And, always, there was that fear at the back of my mind that it could be a child next time.

Both Edd and I contacted the taxi company to try to convince them that there had been a real loss, but there was very little interest. I met with denial, threats, lies and even a grudging acceptance. They admitted that their driver had been in Poole Park Road at the time, and had been driving very fast; however, they claimed that this was because he was taking a passenger to hospital. I checked this with the lady who had witnessed everything and she told me that not only had he been driving in the opposite direction to the hospital, but also that there had been no one else in the car. Their excuse was, according to the police, a confession that their driver had been responsible, but no action could be taken. There was nothing I could do, and that's been one of the most difficult things to deal with.

With any sudden loss, there is the need to blame some-one for the unfairness that takes the loved one from the life of the bereaved. In this situation, I knew who was responsible, and there had even been an admission of it, but still my hands were tied. No one cared. Casper was only a cat.

No, I had to tell myself – that wasn't strictly true. The person who killed him didn't care, but plenty of other people did and it was those good, honest, caring individuals who drew me out of my grief. The global hug I received in the wake of Casper's passing was still holding me close. Every day, letters and emails piled up and each one told a tale of humanity and common purpose. It was humbling and it was so, so helpful. One lady from Australia wrote to me and I replied immediately, sending her some pictures of Casper too; her next letter showed just how important people felt it was to reach out at this terribly sad time.

Dear Sue –

Thank you so much for taking the time to write such a lovely letter. I was very pleased to know that my card reached you as I only had your name and that you lived in Plymouth from the article about Casper in my local paper. It certainly was a surprise as I didn't expect a reply to my card. I just wanted you to know that other people were sad about the loss of Casper. Thank you also for the photographs of him. I took them to work and showed all the girls, and we are all very sad about what happened to him. I am glad that you have decided to leave his photograph on the buses. I think that is a lovely memorial to him, but also I hope that rotten taxi driver sees Casper's photo every day and is reminded of his carelessness and lack of compassion. I am sure he didn't mean to run over him, but if he hadn't been speeding he might have been able to avoid hitting him, and then not to stop to aid him was truly cowardly, and I do not understand how people can be so cruel. The fact that he almost hit a person as well, and that the company won't do anything is just disgusting. It is a pity that the driver can't be forced to own up and apologize. In this city, Adelaide, the law says drivers must stop and call the police if they hit an animal, regardless of what it is; hopefully you might be able to get this law in Plymouth.

By writing his story at least a little bit of good will come out of all the sadness. I see that Casper's You Tube video has been updated; I watched it last night and had a cry. I suppose you wouldn't be able to watch it, but it is a wonderful tribute to him, and I am sure that thousands of people who have seen it are sad as well.

My dear cats were Dolly Cat and Mr Sam. Dolly became ill last July, and I was taking her to the vet every couple of weeks for checks, then in the early hours of 27 September she suddenly died. She would have been eighteen on the 1st of December. Then a couple of days later Mr Sam wouldn't eat, so off to the vet again. The vet discovered a tumour in his bowel. He wasn't in any pain at that time, but there wasn't anything to be done to save him, so it was just palliative care. I was taking him to the vet every two weeks for injections to help his appetite and vitamins. I cherished every minute with him, and worried about him constantly. Then on 13 January I knew that he couldn't go on any longer, so he was put to rest by the vet. He turned sixteen on the 1st of January. It has been heartbreaking to lose them both so close together. I'd had them both since they were kittens and I miss them so much, after all those years. I will eventually get another cat, as life without a furry person around the house is very strange, but I'm too sad at the moment and I need some time to get past the last six months.

Please take care – I hope the pain of losing Casper in such an awful way is easing a little, but as you said it never really goes away, I guess you just find a way of living with it.

Kind Regards – Bronwyn, Australia

All over the world and closer to home, people were being reminded of their losses over the years by Casper's death. A lady called Margaret sent a beautiful card in which she said:

To lose a true friend is never easy – know that you're in my thoughts. I was so sorry to read of the death of Casper. What an amazing cat he was! In these days of nothing but bad news in the papers, it was so enjoyable to read about Casper and his daily bus journey. There will be many people who will be thinking of you at this time.

I believed her. There seemed to be such love sent to me in every mail delivery, including this one:

He was a lovely cat just like my Robert, one I had years ago. When I used to see him, I'd always sit down beside him. After a while I started stroking him and he never seemed to mind. I would have loved to have sat there all day with him and I used to just think through all the little things that were bothering me. When I had Robert, I used to tell him all my worries but I couldn't say these things out loud to this fellow, as people would have thought I was mad. So, I just went through everything in my mind as I was petting him, and he was such a good cat. I'd have loved to have taken him home with me, but I'm far too old for a pet, so it was just nice to see him every so often. He was such a comfort to people, even if they just saw him now and again.

A couple from Nottingham wrote:

We were devastated to hear the very sad news about Casper – he must have been a wonderful cat. What we would have given to have known him. The first we ever heard about him was when we were in Cornwall on holiday in October 2009. We have managed to obtain a beautiful photo of him on the bus, waiting for the doors to open. God bless and take care.

All of these people were loving my cat and caring for him, when I had no idea. A lady from Truro said:

I was heartbroken to read the awful news that your darling cat, Casper, had been run over. I just adore animals, especially cats, and remember so well reading the lovely story about him taking trips on the local buses where you live and what a wonderful character he was. It is a terrible heartbreak to lose them. Your little Casper has become as famous as Dewey! As all us animal lovers know, losing an animal is every bit as heartbreaking as losing a person or a child. The first time I had a little cat run over and killed, I was just devastated. You have to hang onto the fact that they had a kind, happy home and lots of love in their little life, which a lot of animals don't often get. It's been lovely to get to know you, albeit for a very sad reason – nowadays it's all the more heart-warming to get to know kind people in the world.

She was absolutely right – it was heart-warming, and it meant even more because I think we've all been conditioned to believe that we're all alone in the world, that 'softness' is a bad quality and that no one else feels the same way. It's just not true; there are legions of good people out there. Casper proved that.

Debra from Western Australia wrote:

My young daughter and I read the very sad news about your cat, Casper, this morning and I sent an email straight away to the Plymouth Herald. I was so touched by the story of Casper and I wanted to offer you my sincere sympathies and condolences. I also wish to pass on my sympathies to the bus drivers who came to know Casper over the years, who must be equally upset at the news. I understand you received Casper from a cattery? I have a cat as well – he is sixteen now and my family and I love him dearly. I rescued him just one day away from being impounded into a cat home. He's been a mostly-faithful cat to me ever since! I say 'mostly-faithful' because, as you well know with Casper, my cat has an independent streak and has been wont to disappear for many hours at a time.

There were characters all over the world! Helen, a lady from the US, wrote:

I have cried for such a long time over the story of your Casper's death – I thought this was terribly wrong of me for a while, and feel rather silly, but now realize just why he has touched me so much. My family moved over here from England when I was fourteen, and although I loved the sunshine and opportunities, England still felt like home. I loved going home for Christmas – which we tried to do every year, even when I was a teenager and had long since started college. We stayed with a variety of aunts and uncles all over the country, in farms and in towns, and they all had one thing in common. Cats. We had a dog back in America, and I loved him dearly, but there was something about cats that just said 'home' to me. I have many happy memories of curling up on Christmas Day with one of the family pets, wherever we were staying, and probably missed them more than my human relations! As soon as I was old enough to marry and have my own home, I got a kitten. My husband I have now been married for over twenty years and have

*three children, and both of us ex-pats have always made
sure there's a cat waiting to greet us when we get home.
They've all had terribly English names over the years – we
currently have Percy and Mabel – and I do wonder whether
they are the only things keeping us here. If it wasn't for the
thought of them in quarantine, I would be pushing to come
home, because there was something in Casper's story that
made me so homesick. Was it the buses, or the idea of people
waiting in a queue with a little cat? I'm not sure, but when
I read that he had died, I felt that part of my dream of home
had died too. I hope that you are coping and I hope that
your sad loss does not prevent you getting another cat. You
are in my thoughts.*

Casper had seemed like part of home to me too, and
it was terribly empty, but the letters kept on coming.
Many people offered such reassurances, despite being
strangers with absolutely nothing to gain from offering such kindness. It has made me reconsider so many
things, and I take that as a lesson from Casper. The experience with my son, Greg, and his gran had shown me
that strange things can happen and I now feel that there
is often something to be gained from even the darkest
times.

That's not to say that his death doesn't still hurt. There
are moments when I experience pain where I haven't
expected it. For example, I still look out at the dustbins
thinking I'll see him there. For the first few days after
he died, there was a plastic carrier bag wedged under

the hedge across the road. My mind played tricks on me in my grief, and I sometimes thought it was him. Acceptance is so hard.

If I heard Cassie's disks jingling, it would be so wonderful. It would be just what I needed to convince me that animals have souls, but until then I'm still not sure. His personality and character and what he left behind have certainly left their mark, but perhaps I'm still too emotionally raw to take it to the next stage and think about whether he is still, in some way, looking after me.

I've changed so much over the years and found myself again; in the course of doing so, I've had many cats in my life. As I've built myself up again, the cats have contributed to my confidence and my belief in myself. I never think about what they can give me, just what I can give them, but, looking back on it, they have all done so much.

This wonderful relationship that we can have with our animals should never be taken for granted. If only I could have one more minute with Casper, I would make sure that he knew just how much he meant to me while I was blessed to share my life with him. Take that time if you still have the gift of your fellow creatures in your life – hold them, love them and cherish the moments you spend together, for there will never be enough.

CHAPTER 30

Remembering Casper

When I first started to write this book, I was a little over-whelmed at the prospect. I had never attempted such a thing before but the publishers were very supportive and felt Casper's story was one that would speak to so many people that I felt it was the right thing to do. I made that decision only after thinking very carefully about everything that has happened. The one question that I kept asking myself time and time again was: how could one little cat have made such an impact?

Over the months since Casper's travels had become known, I had received letters, emails and messages from across the globe, all of them full of kindness. This one cat had touched people. He had ignited a spark of some-thing – perhaps love, perhaps recognition – that made it clear to me that we all have much more in common than maybe we realize.

We spend so much time hearing and reading about such awful things – wars, crime, people hating each other and doing terrible things. What Casper's story has made me remember is that there is a lot of good in people. When things are difficult, our natural instinct is to reach out to each other, even when the other person is a complete stranger living on a different continent. If Casper has made two people talk to each other on a bus, or strike up a conversation over a newspaper article, or chat over the garden fence about that funny little cat who liked to ride on the bus, then I genuinely feel that he has made a difference.

I'm not an overly religious person, but I do believe that all of us have that ability to change things – whether we're a person or a cat or anything in between. When I realized just how much Casper had meant to people, many of whom had never even met him, I decided that I had a duty to make sure that his whole story was told. I only hope that by sharing these words I can give some comfort to people who have lost their own pets, and make them realize that they aren't alone.

I spent many happy hours remembering my lovely Casper, and all the cats who went before him. The whole process reminded me of things I thought I'd forgotten. It made me find out more about this funny little cat who'd managed to construct a world of his own every day. I went to the bus depot to talk to all the lovely drivers and company staff who had known Casper and had helped; I spoke to neighbours and passengers who had known him well; I met people through Facebook and other sites who all had stories to share.

It all started to make sense to me at that point, as I found out more and more about my own cat and his secret life. I also realized that people were waiting for an opportunity to talk, not just about him, but about the animals they had loved and lost. It was as if Casper gave them an excuse to be honest about their feelings.

If you are reading this because you, too, have lost a beloved pet, please take comfort in the fact that you experienced a wonderful relationship with them. Yes, the pain of losing them is awful, and you may feel that you simply can't go on without them, but you will. And the reason I believe you will is that loving makes us stronger. Through sharing our hearts and hopes, we expand our capacity to care. Don't feel ashamed by your emotions, don't think that you have to close yourself off and never discuss or remember the creature who brought you so much pleasure, for what would be the point of the pain if we didn't sometimes allow ourselves a shred of happiness?

If you are reading this because you think that previous bereavements have been too much to bear and that you cannot risk more hurt, then please remember all the cats I've lost over the years. If I had taken that approach, I would never have known Casper; I would never have had the strength to bring him into my life. If that had happened, there would have been thousands upon thousands of people who would never have known his story and taken joy from it. Grief and the fear of being hurt again can be powerful emotions, which can prevent us from doing what our hearts truly desire. If you love animals, don't deny yourself the love and company they bring.

One person emailed me a beautiful poem, written by her eleven-year-old son, who had wanted to let me know how Casper had affected him. This is what he sent me:

> *Casper was a lovely cat*
> *As proud as proud can be.*
> *How I wish I could have seen*
> *Him on the number 3.*
>
> *Each day he had a journey*
> *Which took him near and far*
> *Always on his favourite bus*
> *Not by paw or car!*
>
> *I would have loved to meet him*
> *I'd hold him and I'd say:*
> *'Oh Casper, you are beautiful,*
> *Please don't go out today.'*
>
> *I'd keep him close beside me*
> *And when that car went by,*
> *I'd be so happy Casper lived*
> *That day he did not die.*
>
> *For I have lost my own dear cats*
> *And still I miss them so*
> *Each day I think about them*
> *And wish they did not go.*

But cats are independent
We have to let them stray
And cross our fingers that they will
Come back to us one day.

This is what I pray for you
Though the tears still burn
Love will find its way back home
And Casper will return.

Yet again I was in floods of tears as I read it but they were tears of happiness and acceptance too. Casper had changed my life, but he had left it. I'd never be the same again, nor would many, many people who had been touched by him. What a marvellous legacy for anyone, never mind one little fluffy rescue cat.

It is many weeks now since Casper died, even though it feels like yesterday. I still miss him so much. You never mend really and the hurt doesn't go away but you adapt somehow. We have been left with a huge void despite the other cats, whom I love dearly. I've never wanted Casper's death to be in vain. All I could think of to begin with was of the many animals out there who desperately need help. There will come a time when I do share again, when I feel that there is more love to go around, but at the moment my memories of Casper and those who went before him are enough.

For now.

Epilogue

There are so many little things that I miss about you, Casper. I would love to be able to write you a poem, but that isn't my talent. All I can do is speak from the heart, the heart that still has your paw prints firmly stamped upon it.

Even though between my children, sisters, brother and myself we have twenty-one rescue cats under our care, I miss the comfort I felt hearing the jingle of your collar disks as you trotted along, knowing that you were safe and couldn't be too far away if I could hear the sound.

I miss not having to put every scrap of food away in the kitchen, as you were such a dreadful thief. I'd happily have you take whatever you wanted all day long just to have the joy of you back in my life again.

I miss you sitting on the worktop watching me make meals, desperately hoping that a tasty morsel would find its way to you – as it somehow always did.

I miss the way you always had the energy and love to

run up and greet me when I got home, no matter how late or early it was, no matter what had been going on in your day or mine.

I miss seeing you sit on the dustbin by the front window, watching the world go by as if there were no finer place to be and no finer pageant to watch.

I miss looking out the bedroom window and laughing as I spotted you sitting in the queue with the other passengers waiting for the bus as if it was the most natural thing in the world.

I miss buying your treats and the closeness as we sat on the sofa together in the evening, content with the world, content with the simple pleasures of life.

What would I give to have one last cuddle? So much, so much – but life goes on, and nothing can bring you back, so I can only make a promise to you, which is to recognize all that you gave me and spread your message.

What did I learn from Casper?

Enjoy life.

Take pleasure in the simple things – sunshine, turkey roll and a bus ride might not be what works for you, so find your own recipe for a good life and stick to it.

Find something you love to do and keep doing it.

Believe that the world is a good place full of good people, and you might just find out that you're right.

That last piece of advice might surprise some people because, were it not for a bad thing done by a thoughtless person, Casper would be here today. However, he taught me something else: good can come from bad. The last few years have been hard ones, but in the middle of it all, it was almost as if Casper decided that he was going to give something to us. His spirit of adventure and love of travel meant that, somehow, he reached out to the world and the world responded. His life brought out something in people – but his death brought out even more. I would never have known how kind strangers could be, how much comfort you could get from someone you'd never met, but each day brings another letter, more caring words, and it's as if Casper is speaking to me, telling me to hold on, to be brave and to keep his memory alive.

So, thank you, Casper, thank you so much – until we meet again.

My Story Continued

Casper

🐾

So, is my story a happy one or a sad one?

Forgive me for saying so, but I think only a human would ask that question.

We all have our time. And my time with my mum, with you all, had come to an end.

I had a life before Sue and before the story you've just read, and there were moments in that life that taught me much about the ways of the world. In learning all my tricks, I discovered a whole new existence and enjoyed a fabulous set of adventures. But dwelling on things long gone is of no benefit to man or beast. I had fun. I got into some scrapes. While the manner in which things ended was sad, I can't complain - although if I'm lucky enough to have a next time, I'll avoid those horrible speeding metal boxes that aren't nice friendly buses.

No life is without its troubles, but that means we should take time to appreciate the good things when they come along - and you humans would do well to relax more often.

Take time to enjoy the beauty around you. Enjoy a sunny day but see the joy in the raindrops too. Think how delightful the flowers are but know that the weeds and bushes also have their place. They provide marvellous cover for us cats when we want to watch the world go by. Everything has a place; everything has good in it, if you take a moment to find it.

As I bask in the sunshine on the rainbow bridge I want to impart some final words of wisdom from a feline who knew what it was like to be given a second chance. Appreciate what you have, seize love where you find it and always, always, take a moment to admire a beautiful cat as he or she walks by. For, who knows, that cat might have something to teach you . . .

With love - Casper

Acknowledgements

My sincere thanks to Linda Watson-Brown, who was so patient with me and helped me to write such a lovely book. To all the staff at Simon & Schuster UK, who made the book possible in the first place. To all at First Group, especially Karen Baxter and the Number 3 bus drivers, who took such great care of Casper when he took his bus trips.

About the author

Susan Finden was a cat lover from an early age – as a little girl, her first pet, Blackie, had helped her through some difficult times, such as the tragic death of her sister from cancer. She knew from that stage that, when she had her own family, she would do all she could to make animals a central part of a happy home life. As a mother-of-three, she made sure that cats played an important role in her children's lives – instilling in them a love of animals which remains to this day. As time went on, Susan's feline friends remained with her and grew in number as she took in rescue cats. When Susan remarried, she continued to adopt unloved animals from around the country. At a rescue home in Weymouth, Susan came across Casper, and from that point her life was changed for ever. Susan continues to take in rescue cats today and has plans to adopt again in the near future.

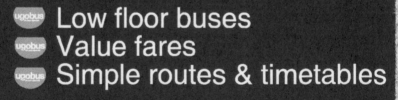